How to plan the

·NATIONAL·

CURRICULUM

in the primary
classroom

*Ruth Merttens* · *Jeff Vass*

Heinemann Educational,
a division of Heinemann Educational Books Ltd,
Halley Court, Jordan Hill, Oxford OX2 8EJ

Oxford   London   Edinburgh
Melbourne   Sydney   Auckland
Ibadan   Nairobi   Gaborone   Harare
Kingston   Portsmouth NH (USA)
Singapore   Madrid   Bologna   Athens

First published July 1990

ISBN 0 435 80617 3

Designed and produced by AMR

Printed and bound in Great Britain
by Richard Clay Ltd, Bungay, Suffolk.

**Dedication**

To Monster
And to all the other children in England and Wales.

**Acknowledgements**

An author tends to lean on a lot of people when writing a book. Two authors tend to lean
on twice as many people! We'd like to record our thanks to Pat Brown, Ros Leather,
Richard Border and Eric Greer, who in their different ways have each given us a lot of help.
We would also like to thank our Head of Department, Dr Greg Condry. Finally, we would
like to thank especially Deborah Curle and Ian Merttens for providing, not least, calm
while we panicked and panic while we were calm!

**References**

4.1    The IMPACT Project (1989) Complete Resource Pack; London, IMPACT-PNL.

5.1    DES/WO (1989) English in the National Curriculum, (Interim Document) NCC
       HMSO.

5.2    Pye, J., 'Invisible Children' (1988) OUP.

5.3    Bossert, S., Classroom Task Organisation and Children's Friendships in 'Children in
       Their Primary Schools: A New Perspective' Ed Pollard. Pollard, A., (1985) Cassell.

5.4/5.5    Merttens, R. and Vass, J., 'Special Needs in Maths' in 'Tackling Learning
       Difficulties' Ed. Robinson, O., Thomas, G., (1988) Hodder and Stoughton.

5.6    Merttens, R. amd Vass, J., (1987) IMPACT – a learning experience; Primary Teaching
       Studies, 2, No.3, pp263-272.

5.7    Topping, K., and Wolfendale, S., (1985) Parental Involvement in Children's Reading,
       Beckenham, Croom Helm.

5.8    DES/WO (1989) Science in the National Curriculum, NCC HMSO.

6.1    DES (January, 1989) Education Reform Act 1988: Information requirements
       relating to the school curriculum and its assessment. Draft Circular.

# Contents

# *Introduction -*
# *New signposts*

IMAGINE waking up to find that, overnight, someone had changed all the familiar road-markings, street-signs, traffic-light systems and other conventions by which we navigate around our environment. Let us further imagine that new and strange road-markings and lights had replaced the old ones. Getting about would be made temporarily difficult.

There are two things we can use to find our way about. Firstly, we can still use landmarks that have always been there like trees, pubs and monuments. Secondly, we can start to learn the **rules** by which the new system operates: every time you see a red circle you are being warned about something; green triangles indicate toxic chemicals and so on.

You will also need a guide, a survivor's guide. You will need to know not only how the new rules fit together but also how they relate to your particular environment.

The Education Reform Act, commonly referred to as ERA, has brought about changes to the familiar landscape of education no less revolutionary than those in our imaginary situation above. In September 1989 when teachers of infants went back into schools, they found themselves having to use a new language to talk about teaching and learning. The subject matter they had previously taught in their own way was now re-arranged into a new format. There had been very little time for preparation.

The landscape of teaching and learning in England and Wales now has not only new landmarks but also the equivalent of a completely different Highway Code. In order to plan our own routes across this altered landscape we must have familiarity not only with our local landmarks but also with the language and layout of the Code-book.

## ▢ Our approach

We, the authors of this book, like any guides, have a particular approach to the territory in which we set ourselves up as guides. The approach we have taken reflects our involvement in writing curriculum materials, designing record-keeping and assessment systems and delivering National Curriculum In-Service Training in the schools of 17 Local Education Authorities between Humberside and Devon inclusively.

Although schools are required to implement a 'National' curriculum, it is clear that each Local Education Authority (LEA) is taking **different approaches** to how it implements this curriculum. Indeed, schools within the same authority are taking different approaches from each other in how they are setting about delivering the new curriculum.

It is clear that some aspects of the National Curriculum are relatively flexible. Schools are discovering this while handling the **details** of the curriculum. But, other aspects of the new arrangements are **fixed**. The fixed aspects remain relatively hidden beneath a welter of documents. This is sad because it is the more fixed features of the curriculum which, when taken together, give us a picture of the overall pattern. A vantage point which would enable us to plan.

This indicates a very important fact about the National Curriculum, one which is fundamental to our approach. It boils down to this: the National Curriculum is:

1  a **framework** of **fixed** standards, and procedures of assessment and reporting;
2  an **entitlement** of children to a specific set of skills and knowledge we call 'curriculum content'. A **variety** of methods may be adopted to deliver this entitlement.

The National Curriculum **framework** refers to the 'matters, skills and understanding' that children acquire in school. Such things as:

- being able to count to 20;
- knowing that Claudius Caesar ordered the invasion of Britain in 43 AD;
- understanding why it rains.

The **content** that children are entitled to can be changed by the government minister in charge of the education service. The **methods** of **delivering** this entitlement are free to vary from school to school and teacher to teacher.

We feel that it is essential that everybody has a shared picture of the overall **framework** of the National Curriculum and the **standard** processes that it sets up. Only by having a grasp of the 'whole', so to speak, can we plan **our own** routes effectively across the new terrain.

## About this book

The book is arranged so that we deal with National Curriculum vocabulary and we get an overall grasp of the **framework** in the first two chapters.

### Let's speak the same language...

Chapter One looks at the vocabulary of the new curriculum. Much of this will already be familiar to most teachers; on the other hand, many of the new words and phrases, for example 'Attainment Targets', have remarkably different usages up and down the country. So, this chapter irons out the differences. Where an interpretation of a word or phrase has been made by schools or LEAs, we have compared the interpretation to the least flexible meaning that can be given it by the National Curriculum framework.

### Let's get a bird's-eye view of the landscape . . .

Chapter Two sketches the main features of the National Curriculum framework in **outline**. We describe each feature briefly so that we achieve a 'birds-eye view' all can share. A grasp of the framework in outline is necessary to **any** effective teaching programme or classroom organization.

## Teaching and assessing in the new framework...

Chapters Three, Four and Five set out forms of classroom organization that can be employed in practice. We look in detail at what National Assessment and record-keeping mean in the classroom. We look at the implications that these have for classroom materials in how we view them, create them, assess with them and choose them.

We provide strategies and examples based on the following features:

- ❏ Planning
- ❏ Classroom activities
- ❏ Different teaching approaches
- ❏ Record-keeping
- ❏ Continuous assessment
- ❏ Standard Assessment Tasks (SATs)
- ❏ Assessment-based organization of classroom materials

## Reporting back...

Chapter Six discusses one of the most important changes made in the practice of education in England and Wales. Built into the framework of the National Curriculum is a complex process of **reporting**.

The reporting process will ensure that detailed information about the assessment of children and the school's delivery of the curriculum will be reported routinely to parents, LEAs and the Government.

Reporting is not simply letting parents and others know how the children are measuring up against the standards set out in the National Curriculum framework. The act of reporting is itself an integral part of the on-going assessment of children. The reported information will be used in a number of ways by external agencies such as the LEA.

We look at **what** information needs to be produced by:

- ❏ teachers;
- ❏ governors;
- ❏ Local Education Authorities.

We examine **where** this information goes and **how** it is to be presented.

## Changes...

Almost daily we hear of some change about to be made to the National Curriculum. At least, rumours abound about 'changes of direction', 'U-turns', 'SATs for seven-year olds are going' and so on. The new curriculum has not even had time to gather dust on staffroom shelves before we hear that major revisions may be in the pipe-line.

It may seem, therefore, slightly perverse to be offering advice about teaching within a 'National Curriculum Framework' that changes as frequently as the weather. For example, the prospect that teachers will have to 'moderate' (see page 15) their assessments of children now looks much less likely than it did eighteen months ago.

The view taken in this book, however, is that any such changes which may **appear** drastic do not actually affect the **basic mechanisms** put into place by the ERA. We take the view that moderation, SATs for seven-year olds as well as continuous assessment could all **go** without affecting either the fundamental structure of the National Curriculum or the effects it is likely to have on education in England and Wales.

The purpose of this book is to give teachers a sense of the underlying structure of the National Curriculum together with examples of its principles in operation in the classroom.

CHAPTER ONE

# The key terms

## Let's speak the same language

### The National Curriculum Instruction Manual...

It is rare to find a book about teaching and learning in which the very first chapter has to set out a list of new words and phrases it intends to use throughout. It is more usual to find such a thing when you unpack a new computer or fridge. With computers and fridges things will fail to work if you do not follow the jargon accurately.

The National Curriculum is a complex piece of machinery. Like a machine, all its parts fit together in such a way that if you took out one piece the rest would not work. Just as 'software' becomes meaningless without the term 'hardware', so does the phrase 'Attainment Target' become useless without the notion of 'Levels of Attainment'.

The National Curriculum is a curriculum, assessment and reporting **package**. We must view it as a complete package. There is a very strong tendency to become lost in the **detail** of various bits of the National Curriculum. This has led to over-estimating the value of one bit, for example, the content of certain Attainment Targets, over the value of another, for example 'Programmes of Study'.

Recall the famous elephant which had three blind men attempting to discover what it was. One man had the trunk, one had the tail and one was holding the elephant's leg. Each man thought he had a true picture of the whole.

Your own involvement with the National Curriculum will put one part of it nearer to you than other parts. The consequence of this is that the part we call 'Attainment Targets' will be seen from one perspective by a teacher, and from a very different perspective by someone working wholly in assessment.

This chapter goes on firstly to say how things have changed; and secondly, to take each 'part' of the National Curriculum in turn. Each part will be considered in its relation to the whole package. This does not invalidate what you may already know about, say, Attainment Targets. Our concern is to show them in broader perspective.

## From the old to the new...

Let's start by considering how the old approach to the curriculum has altered.

It has been said that the old curriculum was a bit like a large bag with many different activities, topics and subjects in it.

**Fig. 1.1**

The job of the teacher then was to take out and select various items from the bag and arrange them in a particular order for the children in the class. The National Curriculum still requires teachers to select items from the bag, but the organization of the items in the bag has changed.

The National Curriculum has cleared a space in the bag into which has been put certain items: now called 'core' and 'foundation' subjects.

The purpose of this is to ensure that teachers give priority to items in this part of the bag first.

For the sake of organization each item, each activity has been broken up into columns called 'Attainment Targets'. Many such columns add together to form a 'subject' such as maths or science. The Attainment Target columns do not contain complete descriptions of things to do in the classroom. They state what units of skill and knowledge children need to be taught in order to be said to 'cover' an area called 'number' in maths or 'living things' in science.

**Fig. 1.2**

This is the view most teachers have of Attainment Targets:    that they are **portions** of the curriculum.

This is true. But the space in the bag containing these Attainment Target 'columns' has been organized 'horizontally' into **levels** as well. This means that any classroom activity plucked from the National Curriculum space in the bag is not only located by subject but also by level **within** specified regions of that subject.

So, the **content** of the curriculum, the old 'body of knowledge', has been located within columns and again on **levels**. It is this organization of the **content** of the curriculum which forms the basis of the National Curriculum **framework**. This organization into columns (Attainment Targets) and levels is the basis of all the **processes** The National Curriculum sets in motion.

The National Curriculum is both a description of a body of knowledge **and** a vehicle for assessing the delivery of that body of knowledge.

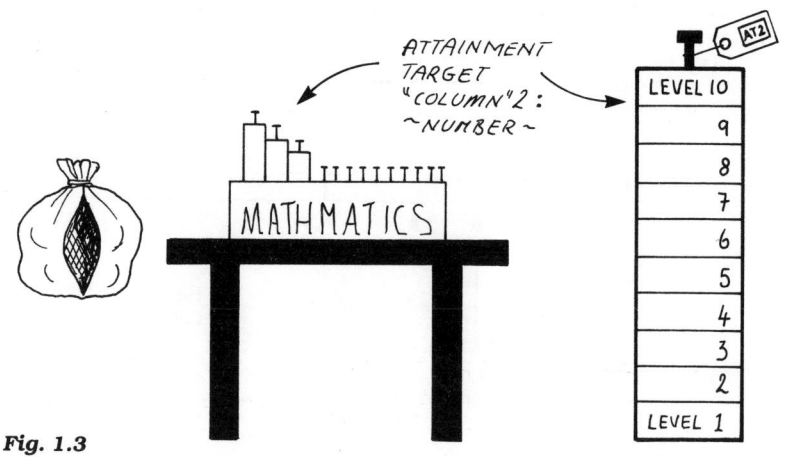

**Fig. 1.3**

It is simultaneously a description of the curriculum content and a process of assessment. We can therefore discuss both **content** and **process**.

## 1 *National Curriculum content*

The **content** of the new curriculum is sometimes referred to as the 'matters, skills and understanding' which children between 5 and 16 are 'entitled' to. This is the 'body of knowledge' we have mentioned. This is what we traditionally think of as all those things children have to learn, all the ground which teachers are expected to cover. The National Curriculum has not introduced any great changes to curriculum content.

As far as National Curriculum content is concerned, we have very little more to say. The radical changes that are being wrought within the education world by ERA almost entirely concern **process**.

## 2 *National Curriculum process*

The **process** of the new curriculum concerns all those means by which the content is delivered, assessed and reported upon. This book is all about the processes of the National Curriculum.

National Curriculum process can be subdivided, very broadly, into **Programme of Study** and **Key Reporting Age**.

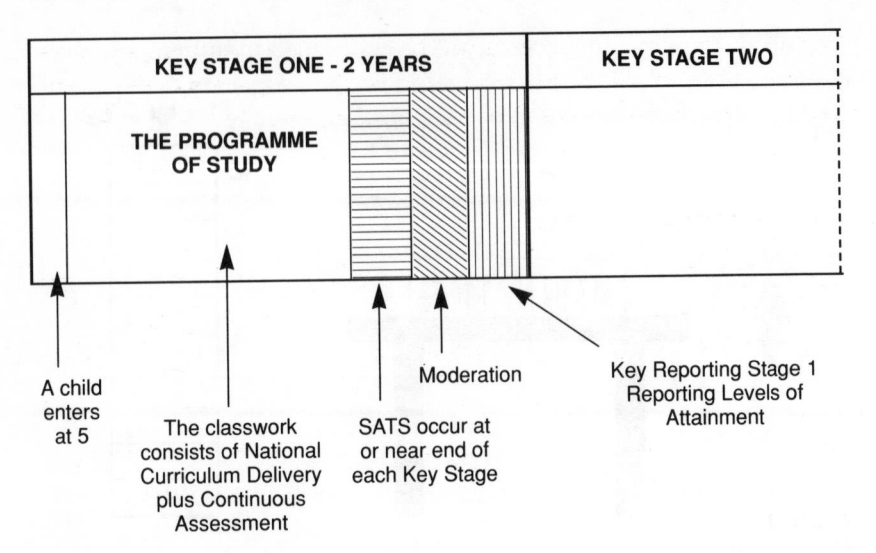

*Fig. 1.4*

## 3 Programme of Study

Figure 1.4 shows that children at 5 receive a Programme of Study which:

**a)** delivers a curriculum entitlement - that is to say, provides them with the curriculum content which they must cover at this stage in their education;

**b)** describes their Levels of Attainment - that is to say, enables teachers (or parents or anyone else) to specify at which level a child is working in each subject.

## 4 Key Reporting Ages

At these points the child's attainments are summarized to enable us to inform parents of progress as well as to indicate how the school as a whole is doing.

## 5 Progression

Figure 1.4 illustrates the broad definition of 'progression' referred to by **politicians**. Progression under ERA is simply the movement through the following steps: Programme of Study, Standard Assessment Tasks and Reporting.

However, teachers and parents will be concerned to understand progression in terms of shorter time periods. This suggests the frequent and continuous assessment of each child.

## 6  Key Stages

The periods between Key **Reporting** Ages are referred to as **Key Stages**. For example, the National Curriculum Council (NCC) refers to the period that children occupy between 5 and 7 as the **First Key Stage**.

The Second Key Stage is the period from 7 to 11, the Third Key Stage is from 11 to 14 and the Fourth Key Stage is from 14 to 16.

## 7  Attainment Targets

The National Curriculum has divided up the substance of the curriculum into portions known as Attainment Targets. There are at present 6 Attainment Targets in English, 14 in maths and 17 in science.

An Attainment Target is a specified portion of the curriculum defined in the ERA as those things a child ought to know and be able to do because they have an entitlement to be taught them.

## 8  Levels of Attainment

Any Attainment Target is divided into 10 levels. For example, Attainment Target 2 in science is called 'The Variety of Life'. If children have achieved Level 3 they will 'be able to recognize similarities and differences among living things'. If they have achieved Level 9, however, they will 'understand that food production involves the management of ecosystems, for example, the North Sea in relation to fish stocks, or the creation of artificial ecosystems, for example, farms and market gardens, and that such management imposes a duty of care'.

We can imagine a pupil of 16 on Level 3, AT 2 (science) while a pupil of 8 years could be on Level 9 in the same AT. So, a scheme of work in any Key Stage cannot have a pre-determined content for any child.

## 9 Statements of Attainment

Instead of listing every single skill and fact a child is likely to come across or use in the Attainment Target 'columns', only certain 'special' ones are listed. These are called **Statements of Attainment**.

For example, 'Count, read, write and order numbers to at least 10' is one Statement of Attainment in maths. 'Understand conservation of number' is another. The Statements of Attainment form a single spectrum irrespective of age.

Listing only these 'special' skills is meant to help us do two things. Firstly, when writing plans of classroom activities we refer to these 'statements' so we know what skills we are aiming to achieve at each stage. Secondly, it is by these 'statements' alone that we shall judge a child as 'having' a certain 'Level of Attainment'.

These skills are 'special' only in that they are being used to **define** where the level boundary lines are. They will be used to make **decisions** about where children are operating in each column. They otherwise have no particular merit as compared with other facts and skills a child might master.

> ### Think about it
>
> Each subject area is not only described in Attainment Targets, it is simultaneously divided into 10 Levels of Achievement. This is the major change in the way the curriculum is organized. An Attainment Target is therefore fulfilling two functions:
>
> **a)** It describes a portion of the curriculum content;
>
> **b)** It gives a list of the criteria against which children's performances are to be monitored.
>
> This means that an Attainment Target is telling us which bit of the content we have to teach and at the same time requiring that we use the same set of statements to assess at which level the children are operating.
>
> There is no sensible distinction between a description of what a child has learned and the assessment of that

*learning. Every time we record the activities that a child has done over a given time, we simultaneously and automatically produce an interim assessment of the child.*

*If we say that Fred has done a domino graph, a potato print and a number-line worksheet, and each of these activities is at Level 1, then Fred is recorded as operating at Level 1. In saying what Fred did, we can also say at which level he is performing.*

## 10 Schemes of work

The scheme of work is an individually-tailored syllabus which links the curriculum outlined in the Programmes of Study to the child's Assessment Profile.

In other words, children need a scheme of work to show how they are to cover the content outlined in the teacher's plan for that term and which activities, tasks, worksheets, books, software, etc. they will be using to enable them to work at an 'appropriate level'. The appropriate level is to be found in the child's Assessment Profile.

The teacher is responsible for drawing up an individual scheme of work for each child and for ascertaining that this:

**a)** reflects what is known about the child's level of achievement, and

**b)** indicates **what** strategies and materials will be used to take the child on through **which** Attainment Targets and at stated levels.

## 11 Standard Assessment Tasks (SATs)

These are the externally provided tasks designed to assess the performance of children on a national scale. These tasks will be 'multi-mode' in that they will involve a variety of methods of working on the part of both teacher and child.

SATs will vary in:

**Presentation** - They will be presented to the children by the teacher in a variety of ways - oral, written, pictorial, video, computer, practical demonstration, etc.

**Operation** - The children will need to employ a wide range of methods of working, sometimes writing things down, sometimes working in groups, talking, using calculators or computers, and so on.

**Response** - There will be a variety of means to present answers: written, oral, multiple choice and so on.

## Tasks not tests

SATs are not intended to be like traditional tests. There should be sufficient flexibility within the tasks - some of which may involve work of a project nature - for teachers to be able to incorporate them as a part of normal classroom work.

However, in order to ensure comparability, the marking or grading procedures will be carefully standardized, and the results will need to be moderated across teachers and schools.

## 12 Continuous assessment

The Task Group on Assessment and Testing recommended that National Assessment should be conducted through a **combination** of continuous teacher assessment and Standard Assessment Tasks. The agencies who produce the SATs are required to deliver the mechanisms for this continuous teacher assessment.

Continuous assessment is based on:

a) the teacher's daily or weekly records of what children have done, and
b) observations of specific children, singly and in groups, with attention to particular Statements of Attainment.

It will require the keeping of more systematic and detailed formal records than has hitherto been customary. (See Chapter Three.)

## 13 Performance

The basic unit in any form of assessment is the response of an individual pupil to a particular demand or task. National Assessment stresses that it is not ability, understanding or attitude that is to be assessed. Rather it is what the child can actually **do**.

It is hard, if not impossible, to agree if Jane understands X, or has a concept of Y. But it is relatively easy to discover if she has mastered a specific skill or can perform a certain task.

It is important to remember that in National Curriculum assessment we are focussing upon what children can **do** or demonstrate to us, rather than trying to discover what is going on inside their heads.

## 14 Moderation

Moderation is about 'bringing individual judgements in line with general standards'. All of us tend to be convinced that our assessments of any pupil are accurate and that we are judging by some more or less clear idea of what can be normally expected.

To obtain comparability across schools of LEAs, it is necessary to standardize assessment procedures. It ought not to be easier for a child in Lancashire, for example, to achieve a particular result than it is for a child in Humberside!

The results of the National Assessment system will be moderated mainly through two different methods:

**i)**  Standard Assessment Tasks;
**ii)**  Group moderation.

Group moderation is the only method of standardizing teachers' assessments which permits the professional judgements of teachers to have a **direct effect** upon the conduct of assessment. By coming together in groups across several schools, teachers can discuss differences in their interpretations of what counts as achieving a particular level in a particular Attainment Target.

Teachers can discuss with others, in like positions, methods for obtaining the detailed observations required, and establishing whether a child has achieved a particular Statement of Attainment. These meetings will be vital in helping to establish the teachers' control of the assessment system and preserve some autonomy within the National Curriculum.

## 15 Criterion-referencing

National Curriculum assessment differs from the majority of tests previously and commonly used in schools.

To understand the difference let us consider the analogy of a car MOT test.

A criterion-referenced assessment of a car is based simply on a list of conditions which the car must satisfy to be roadworthy. E.g. Do the indicators work? YES/NO; Is there sufficient tread on the tyres? YES/NO; Are the brakes effective within the defined stopping distances? YES/NO, etc...

A norm-referenced test would look at any car from the point of view of what 'most' cars can actually do. E.g. If most cars have one tyre with insufficient tread, then a car with three good tyres might pass whereas a car with only two good tyres fails. However, the following year 'most' cars may have all four good tyres. Therefore in order to pass the MOT all cars would need to match the norm.

So we may now think of our 'Statements of Attainment' as special skills which are going to act as our **criteria** for deciding where children are on the Levels of Attainment.

## 16 Formative criteria

The Task Group described formative assessment as recognizing the positive achievements of a pupil so that work suitable for the next stage of that pupil's learning may be planned.

The assessment is designed to **supply the information necessary in order to plan the next stages of the pupil's education.**

The outcome of assessment is the identification of **formative criteria.** This is the specific knowledge which helps teachers to plan the appropriate work for the children to do **next**, based upon their discovery of which levels they have achieved in each Attainment Target.

## 17 A summative assessment

The Task Group recommended a means of summing up or summarizing the level reached by each child across a range of Attainment Targets in the subjects studied. The summative assessment of the achievement of each child is reported back to parents, teachers and other concerned professionals at each of the Key Reporting Ages. However, a yearly report is required from all teachers on each of their individual pupils. This will have a summative as well as a formative aspect.

It is accepted that at 16 the focus shifts from being formative to being summative. The assessment components for this stage will be specifically designed for summative purposes.

## 18 Profile Components

For the purposes of reporting back to parents, the Attainment Targets are grouped together into 'Profile Components'. The Profile Components reflect broad areas of subjects and indicate the main 'knowledge, skills and understanding to which the subject gives rise'. Profile Components can be envisaged as bundles similar to Attainment Targets.

For example, in English, there are three Profile Components - Speaking and Listening, Reading and Writing.

Profile Components are used to **report back** on National Curriculum delivery. They are not of concern when it comes to planning the curriculum or drawing up a scheme of work.

As things currently stand the Profile Components for the core subjects of mathematics, English and science consist of:

**Mathematics**
Profile Component 1 - Number, Algebra and Measures
Profile Component 2 - Shape, Space and Handling Data

**English**
Profile Component 1 - Speaking and Listening
Profile Component 2 - Reading
Profile Component 3 - Writing

**Science**
Profile Component 1 - Exploration of Science
Profile Component 2 - Knowledge, Skills and Understanding of Science

When it comes to presenting the results of a child's assessment to parents, the Profile Components are easier to assimilate.

Children's overall achievement can be seen in terms of their performance in various Profile Components. Parents and teachers will want to discuss how children are progressing through each Profile Component, rather than their 'aggregated score' across all the subjects.

## 19 Aggregated distributions

Schools will combine the results of all the pupils in a class to produce a table which gives a picture of their results. For example, it is anticipated that at the first Key Reporting Stage the average distributions will look like this:

| LEVEL | 1 | 2 | 3 |
|---|---|---|---|
| % of 7 year-olds at each level | 10% | 80% | 10% |

*1.5 Anticipated Average Results*

A local school publishing their results might, for example, achieve the following distributions for the first Key Stage:

| LEVEL | 1 | 2 | 3 |
|---|---|---|---|
| % of 7 year-olds at each level | 30% | 60% | 10% |

*1.6 Possible School Result*

Schools **must** publish their distribution of results for Key Stages 2, 3 and 4. They are 'strongly advised' to publish their distributions for the first Key Reporting Stage, but they are not compelled to do so.

The assessments of children will be used to compare teachers, classes, schools and LEAs. The aggregated scores may be used as the basis of evaluation. They will also be used to produce national averages.

Finally...this chapter can be used later as a glossary of terms.

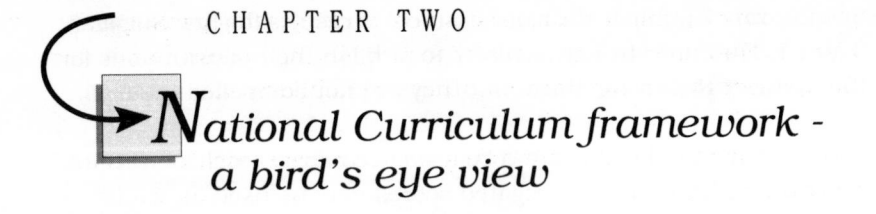

CHAPTER TWO

# National Curriculum framework - a bird's eye view

THIS chapter looks at the processes involved in making the National Curriculum work. Part of the difficulty for those involved in implementing these processes has been the time scale allowed in which to do so. Some of us feel we have scarcely had time to read all the documantation produced, let alone to assimilate and understand it. Many teachers have adopted a minimalist 'coping' strategy. This enables teachers to read or familiarize themselves with each part of the National Curriculum as they meet it in the course of going about normal teaching and school duties.

The problem with 'just coping' is that it is impossible to get a sense of the framework of the National Curriculum. One teacher may know certain sections of the maths document very well, another may know the English document, but no-one sees the thing as a whole. It is hard for teachers, therefore, to appreciate all the implications of some of the documentation, or the repurcussions of decisions made now about seemingly unimportant details.

In this chapter we give a 'bird's eye view' of the National Curriculum. We look at the main components in terms of the role they play in the complete process. At each step we state **briefly** what is expected of schools and teachers. Subsequent chapters deal with the delivery itself.

## A teaching and assessment package

The National Curriculum is not just a giant dictionary of facts and skills which all children in England and Wales have to be taught and which they will have to be tested on periodically. The National

Curriculum is a curriculum, assessment and reporting **package**. The layout of Attainment Targets affects the way SATs are designed; Profile Components affect the way assessments of children are reported.

The following diagram illustrates the framework of the National Curriculum.

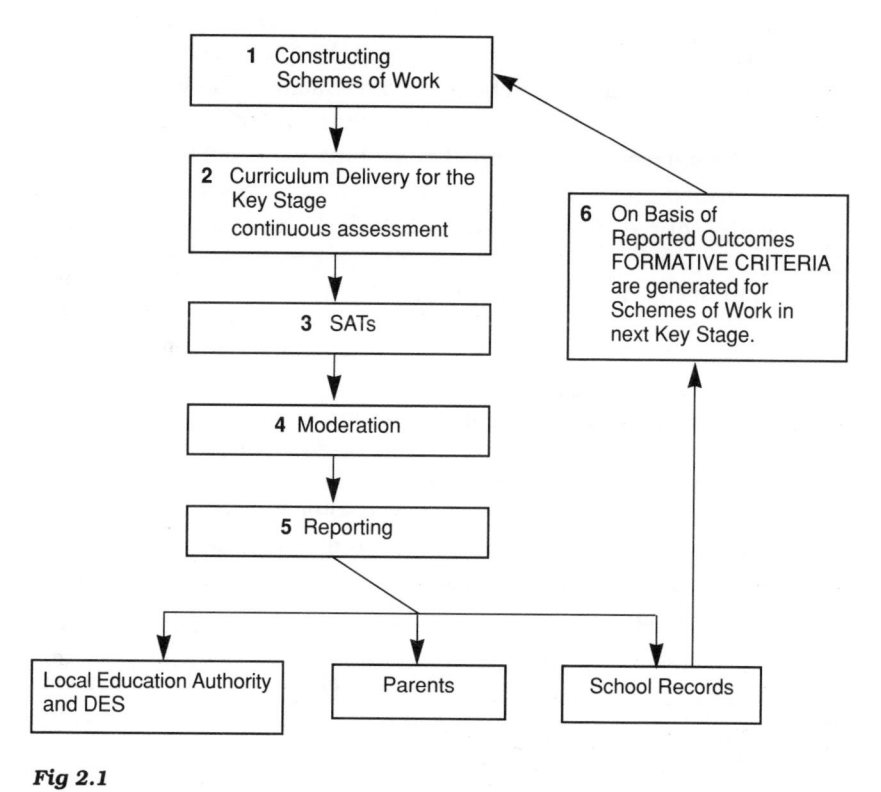

**Fig 2.1**

## National Curriculum framework - step by step

We will now work through the diagram pausing to make brief comments on each step.

### 1 Schemes of work

The first point to make about a scheme of work is that it is something which applies to an individual child. This means that, at first sight, a teacher is responsible for drawing up 30 or more schemes of work, one for each child in a class. In practice, a scheme of work for an individual child can best be thought of as the mapping of the child's route through the teachers' more general classroom plan. The precise steps for generating schemes of work are outlined in Chapter Three.

The second point to note about a scheme of work is that it is both the starting and end point of assessment. It is the 'plan of campaign' for each child's individual work schedule from which the activities, tasks, worksheets, etc. which the child actually does are drawn. But it becomes the subject of alteration after we have assessed how children have performed on their work so far. Thus it is the scheme of work which is the source of the classwork on which the assessment of the child is based. And it is the scheme of work which must be adapted in the light of the results of that assessment.

## 2 Classwork - curriculum delivery

The Programmes of Study outline **what** is to be taught. Together with the non-statutory guidance, they also give some indication of **how** the curriculum is to be delivered. The classroom tasks, the activities you devise, the worksheets or books you use, the software and videos you select, are your **means** of delivering the curriculum.

For example, in a vertically-grouped infant class, all the children will be at different points in a two-year journey through Key Stage 1. In that two-year journey there will be 6 terms or 12 half-terms. It is necesary to have an overview of the work which is to be done through-out the six half-terms as well as a more or less detailed plan of an immediate term or half-term.

We can think of each chunk of time to which a detailed scheme of work applies as being a sequence of classwork sessions, each containing a number of tasks and activities. What we are going to do is to keep a **record** of these tasks and activities and make **teacher-assessments** on the basis of them.

We have traditionally made a distinction between records and assess-ment like this:

❏ We have a record of which activities the child has **done** (record-keeping);

❏ We have a record of what the child has learned or where they have got to (assessment).

The National Curriculum removes this distinction. The content of the curriculum is described in 10 levels. Any activity that the child does can be calibrated against these levels. This means that if I look back over a record of **what** a child has done over the last term or half-term, I have an automatic record of the **level** at which he or she **appears** to be operating. Thus, the records I keep provide a series of interim and provisional assessments of each child.

You are obliged, under the terms of ERA, to supply quite specific information to individual parents, other colleagues, the school, and finally, to the LEA and the DES. In addition you need to record, probably more systematically and certainly more formally than previously, the learning experiences of the children for assessment purposes as described above.

The Schools Examinations and Assessment Council is giving all teachers the means to continuously monitor the progress of each child. These will focus on specific Statements of Attainment and enable you to ascertain what the child has achieved according to National Curriculum standards. At the time of writing, the SEAC advice comes in the form of two packs, Packs A and B, and a Sourcebook C.

The continuous assessment will enable you:

**a)** to see what progress children have made over a period of time;

**b)** to see whether the work they are being given is at an appropriate level;

**c)** to make formal **decisions** about where a child is on the Attainment Target levels.

Together with the assessment obtained by recording the experiences a child has, these teacher assessments will make up the assessment profile for each child.

The National Curriculum tells us **what** ground we have to cover.

Although guidance is given, it does not tell us precisely **how**. Each teacher is left to decide:

❑ how the classroom is to be organized;
❑ which Attainment Targets are to be covered and in what order;
❑ how much of the work is of an integrated nature;
❑ the teaching methods - group work, individualized work, class teaching - on a day-to-day basis, as well as a matter of long-term strategy;
❑ how much time you can devote to each subject within the National Curriculum;
❑ which children will do which tasks/work;
❑ which schemes and resources you will use.

Of course, many of these are matters for whole school policy rather than being the subject of an individual teacher's decision. However, within the limitations imposed by working in a particular school with particular colleagues, the class teacher remains autonomous in these areas.

## 3 Standard Assessment

SEAC is required to provide a bank of SATs. At or near the end of each Key Stage a number of SATs will be administered to children of 7, 11, 14 or 16. For children of 7 the teacher will be expected to administer three SATs of which one will be administered to **all** 7 year-olds in the country. Four SATs are expected to be undertaken at 11. At 11, 14 and 16 SATs will increasingly reflect the subject boundaries of core and foundation subjects.

The Standard Assessment Tasks should not be thought of as tests. They will consist of a number of inter-related tasks and activities and will last for anything from one week to three weeks, depending upon the final design selected by SEAC and the SAT chosen by the school.

The Task Group recommended that the SATs would be, as far as possible, indistinguishable from normal classwork.

SATs are crucial to the machinery of the National Curriculum. They will determine how we make decisions about a child's Level of Attainment. We may disagree with the results of a SAT assessment on any particular child, but it is the SAT which sets out the ground-rules upon which agreement and disagreement is arbitrated and finally decided.

Continuous assessment is crucial on a daily basis for taking a child through the curriculum. But teacher assessment is bound to be highly variable in the way it is practised and interpreted. So SATs are supposed to help standardize the assessment profiles across classes, schools and LEAs.

SATs have been designed to stand alone as a form of assessment should they have to.

> ### Think about it
>
> Schools will have some control over the final design of SATs since they will make choices as to which SATs from an item bank they prefer. If, after a period of, say two years, it is found that teachers are choosing one type of SAT rather than another, it is probable that the design of the tasks themselves will be modified to take account of this.
>
> What 'normal classwork' is in one classroom, in one school and in one LEA, is highly 'abnormal' classwork in another school, in another LEA. It is difficult to see how, without maintaining a bank of very different SATs, where the 'merging' with normal classwork recommended by TGAT will occur. If the design and mechanisms of the SATs differ from one SAT to another, as this implies, the demand for standardization will fall heavily upon the moderation exercise.

## 4 Moderation exercise

Moderation means making an **adjustment** to assessments which teachers have made during the hurly-burly of the classroom. Teachers are used to making adjustments to their assessments of children since they do just this on a more or less daily basis as a part of normal teaching. As teachers are giving children work, they are simultaneously monitoring their progress and making the necessary adjustments to their assessments in the light of what other teachers in other schools contribute. The moderation process will be in three stages:

1   We need to review a child's progress regularly and systematically. You will need to 'moderate' your estimations of a child at the end of each period to which a detailed scheme of work applies. This will, in practice, be termly or half-termly in most primary schools, and termly and yearly in most secondary schools. This will involve you in discussions with other staff in the school. It will mean teachers spending time in each other's classrooms and observing each other's assessments of children. The assessments, and each teachers' means of making those assessments, will need to be discussed in a series of staff meetings. This is the continuous assessment process. Detailed advice and arrangements are outlined in SEAC Pack B.

2   After SATs have been administered, you will have for any child two sets of estimates of where the child is on each Attainment Target attempted in terms of levels. One set of estimates comes from continuous assessment, together with your own records. The second set of estimates comes from the SATs. In the light of SATs, you may want to 'moderate' your own estimates.

3   A 'moderation exercise' is planned in which teachers take their SAT and continuous assessment results to a moderation group consisting of teachers from anywhere between 15 and 20 schools. In these groups teachers will sit with pieces of work from the children and come to a more standardized and uniform estimation of where their own children are. It will be very important that teachers not only keep their formal records up-to-date and regular, but that they continuously collect evidence of the children's work. Through discussion at these moderation meetings, systematic over-or under-estimation of any children's level of achievement should be eliminated.

At the end of Key Stage 1, for example, it is expected that 80% of 7 year-olds in the country will be at Level 2 in most Attainment Targets. So, moderation groups will be concerned to:

a)   establish a mutual understanding and agreement about the performances of children against the criteria of Level 2 performance in the content documents, and

**b)** establish the means, with guidance from SEAC and NCC, for discerning performances which fall predominatly on either side of Level 2. Current estimates project that this will involve 20% of all 7 year-olds in our example.

## 5 Reporting back

Step 5 involves much more than providing a yearly report for parents. ERA has fundamentally altered the nature, form and purpose of reporting back. From now on, reporting back is a fundamental part of the schooling process. Reported assessment information and associated data will go to three major groups as a matter of course.

### a) Parents

Parents will receive detailed information in the 'school prospectus' about the Programme of Study that their child will be following. They will have right of access to information kept in school such as the detailed scheme of work which teachers produce during their planning for the year ahead.

In addition to the yearly reports, parents will also receive assessment reports at the end of each Key Stage. These reports will contain information on their child's Level of Attainment in each Profile Component together with comparative data on the Levels of Attainment of the rest

**End of Key Stage 1 Report on Levels of Attainment**

|  | SUBJECT | MATHS | | ENGLISH | SCIENCE |
|---|---|---|---|---|---|
|  |  | PC1 | PC2 |  |  |
| Kenneth Butcher Class 4 | Level of Attainment | 2 | 1 |  |  |
| Class Attainment at each level | Level 1 | 5% | 5% |  |  |
|  | Level 2 | 60% | 65% |  |  |
|  | Level 3 | 25% | 30% |  |  |
|  | Level 4 | 10% | 0% |  |  |

**Fig. 2.2**

of the class in those Profile Components. The 'rest of the class' is treated as a group. Parents do have the right to compare their child's results with those of the whole class. The results of one class could be published as a set of distributions. The distributions may be broken down and presented as separate results for each subject or even for each Profile Component.

| Kenneth Butcher Class 4 | Class Attainment | | | | |
|---|---|---|---|---|---|
| | Level | | | | |
| Level of Attainment | 1 | 2 | 3 | 4 | |
| MATHS     PC1...2 | 2 | 22 | 8 | 3 | Numbers of children |
| PC2...1 | 2 | 24 | 9 | – | |
| ENGLISH   PC1...3 | | | | | |

**Fig. 2.3**

There is no question of a 'league table' of named children in any one class or year. But the results of the class as a whole could be presented as numbers of children rather than as percentages.

## b)   The LEA and DES

Both the Local Education Authority and the DES require a great deal more information from schools and in a different format than we have traditionally supplied.

Some of this information concerns such matters as the amount of time you spend on each subject each week. Other parts of the information required will concern the aggregated results of all the assessments.

Parents will have the right of access to all this information and it may be used to make comparisons between schools, teachers, or LEAS in terms of National Curriculum performance.

## c) The school

Each teacher records:

**a)** which Attainment Targets and which levels have been covered during a particular school year;

**b)** which Statements of Attainment each child has achieved throughout that year;

**c)** any topics covered and specific materials used will need to be passed on to the other teachers. In this way the records of individual children and of classwork plans can be used to ensure:

    **i)** that the Programme of Study is adequately delivered over the relevant two or four-year period;

    **ii)** that a complete and continuous assessment profile is maintained for each child;

    **iii)** that there is no unnecessary repetition of children's work, topic, or assessment.

## Conclusion

The National Curriculum is a complete curriculum and assessment package. All the various parts within it, the content documents, the forms for reporting back, etc. make sense only when viewed as part of the larger framework of the whole structure.

While the new curriculum will bring changes to the structure and content of your job, it does **not** dictate **how** you should organize your classroom.

The changes in structure to the education process have been outlined in this chapter in five steps. There will be increasing national uniformity in the ways teachers record, assess and report within this structure.

# CHAPTER THREE

# Assessment and record-keeping

## Introduction

### An integrated system...

We have said that the National Curriculum is a curriculum and assessment package. This means that teachers are responsible for the delivery of the curriculum entitlement and yet are simultaneously responsible for the assessment of children who are acquiring new skills and understanding. In this, and the following two chapters, we will be exploring this novel relationship between learning, teaching and assessing.

This chapter looks at the nature of National Assessment and at the new skills that teachers will need to incorporate into their classroom practice.

Having said that teachers will be getting used to new assessment methods, it should also be said that many of these are **already** in use in many classrooms. The introduction of a national system of assessment will turn these 'tacit' methods into formal and written ones.

Making formal and written assessments regularly means keeping comprehensive records of what children have done and how well they did it. Record-keeping is dealt with towards the end of this chapter. For the moment we shall concentrate on **what** precisely we are meant to assess and keep records about.

### Assessment of performance - seeing is believing...

We reviewed the new words and phrases of the National Curriculum in Chapter One. There we mentioned that National Assessment relies much more on children **demonstrating** that they have skills, rather than on getting children to show they understand some 'concept' which we cannot see first-hand.

It has proved impossible for everybody to agree on a method for showing conclusively that a child has or has not a 'concept of two-ness'. We can, however, describe a set of 'situations' which will help us make judgements for ourselves about a child's skills. For example, we might use the following situations to assess a child:

We can ask a child to:

❑ go to a Lego box and take out 2 bricks;
❑ draw 2 cats;
❑ walk 2 steps.

We cannot make elaborate inferences on the basis of what a child does in these situations. Such 'assessments' are always **thumb-nail sketches** about children's abilities and potentials. But, for the purposes of comparison, we can all agree on some convention. For example, we can all make an agreement that every 5 year-old should be able to follow the instruction 'walk 2 steps', unless some physical reason prevents him.

The skills laid out in the Attainment Targets at each of the 10 levels are just such 'agreements'. Other agreements could have been made, but at the end of the day the ones chosen were thought most appropriate. We call this sort of assessment 'performance-based' because it relies heavily on children actually **doing** things within an agreed framework.

## Making decisions...

These national agreements (about what children should be able to do at any level of the National Curriculum) will be used by the teacher to make curriculum and assessment **decisions**.

The first kind of decision will be to decide how skilled a child already is. This leads to a summative assessment.

The second kind of decision is concerned with what a child should do next. This is a formative assessment.

Note that the first kind of decision involves looking at a child at work within the curriculum in order to make an **assessment**; in the second kind we use an assessment to make a **curriculum** decision.

Chapter Four looks in detail at planning and selecting materials in the classroom on the basis of assessments the teacher has already carried out. Planning a scheme of work and selecting materials are based on formative assessment - they arise as a result of decisions made about what children should be provided with in view of their current performances.

For the rest of this chapter we are concerned only with how we make an assessment decision about a child. This will always involve making a decision about whether a child is **below, at** or **above** any **Level of Attainment**.

Apart from special assessments to determine special educational needs, any assessment carried out in school in future will be about determining **where** children are in any Attainment Target, according to the 10 Levels of Attainment.

## Collecting evidence...

At first sight the job in front of you seems fairly straightforward. In order to be able to assess a child you need to be able to match a child's performance against the nationally agreed, 'standardized list' of skills which we call Statements of Attainment.

In practice one child's performance' will never be exactly the same as any other child's. And even the same child may not do things twice in exactly the same way. In any case classrooms are very busy places. Each day any child will use hundreds of different skills.

By 'visiting' each child in the course of real school activities, you can look to see if any skill observed matches any of those you are looking for.

There are several different ways of going about collecting evidence to make those all-important decisions about levels. Most of these different ways will be utilized by National Assessment in both the following:

❑ Continuous teacher assessment;
❑ Standard Assessment Tasks (SATs).

We now go on to consider in greater detail how the principles discussed in this introductory section will take shape in schools.

## Ways of collecting evidence...

Assessment means making many decisions of the sort:   'Yes, Linda has attained Level 2 in science ATG'. These decisions are important and noteworthy because they will contribute to similar accumulating evidence which will enable the school to supply a mandatory report on Linda's attainment across the National Curriculum at the Key Reporting Age.

The evidence to make and support assessment decisions will come from your own **records** and from SATs.

## Records...

Within the National Curriculum framework you keep a record of two things:

**i)** a record of work done by children in your class, and
**ii)** a record of any formal assessments undertaken in class other than SATs.

The first type is a record simply of what has been covered in class. We describe in detail what these records are about later in this chapter. Briefly, they are concerned with charting our course over the 'terrain' of the curriculum. In themselves they do not involve assessment decisions. For example, if we record that a child has done an activity which involves using skills described in maths AT3 at Level 1, we have **not** asserted that the child successfully used those skills. We say only that a particular activity was done.

The principles of Teacher Assessment have been outlined in the advice given by SEAC in Packs A, B and C.

In any activity a number of skills will be deployed and not all of these will correspond to those listed in Attainment Targets. Those are **special** skills which **define** the **boundary** between one level and the next. For example, in Maths AT 2 'Count, read, write and order the numbers to at least 10' is a level 1 set of skills. A teacher will need to be aware of precisely these specified skills in her observations in order to be able to define a child's level of operation.

Teachers can collect further evidence as to each child's level of performance through a variety of means. These will include:

- ❏ isolating 'key' activities and looking at a child's performance in detail;
- ❏ noting specific and relevant observations of each child as and when they occur in the course of normal classwork.

In targeting 'key' activities it is useful to make a chart listing which of the specified Attainment Target skills the activity demands. As we stated above, a number of the skills deployed by the child during the activity will not be listed in the Attainment Targets and the teacher need only focus upon those which are deemed relevant. It is, in theory at least, then possible to check whether a child has demonstrated mastery of these skills.

## New skills for teachers...

What we have discussed above means that teachers will need new 'assessment skills' themselves. These new skills involve methods of observation, selecting and designing tasks for assessment purposes, 'calibrating' educational materials to the National Curriculum's Attainment Targets, and other techniques which will become a **routine** feature of classwork.

SEAC has produced a set of documents which are supposed to give teachers practice in some of these new techniques. The rest of this chapter investigates:

- ❏ the principles on which SATs are based;
- ❏ how SATs relate to Teacher Assessment;
- ❏ methods for breaking down activities into their component skills;
- ❏ a National Curriculum assessment and record-keeping system.

The following two chapters show the use of these methods in practice.

## Standard Assessment Tasks

### The purpose of SATs

SATs have two broad functions:

**a)** They are supposed to standardize a teacher's best estimates of where children are on the 10 levels in each 'subject' where those estimates have been made during a key stage.
If you have accumulated evidence throughout a key stage, you can make a good estimate about where a child is in each AT in terms of levels. In the absence of your own evidence the SAT will have to do.

**b)** SATs are used everywhere in England and Wales. This means that all children in the country have to demonstrate their mastery of skills (or attainment) in the same or similar tasks.

### SATS differ from previous 'tests'...

SATs are not classroom tests for children. They simply standardize for us, against national benchmarks, how well children are doing within the 10 levels.

There will be a much closer relationship between a SAT and the precise curriculum followed by any school in the future than there has been hitherto between the curriculum and old-style **'tests'**. Both SATs and **any** activity done in **any** classroom at **any** time share an important characteristic:they both come from the same statutory curriculum content arranged in 10 levels.

Standardized tests prior to this have had a much more independent existence. They could not be said to sample the curriculum of a **specific** classroom. They obtained 'scores' of children's work calibrated against a statistically arrived-at norm. This norm is based on quite different assumptions about children's performances in relation to what they might be **expected** to know. A test's expectations of what a child might, or might not, know need have borne no relation to the curriculum actually followed by the children on whom it was used.

## SAT-THINK: *Determine where children are and what they do next*

To understand SATs more clearly, and, indeed, all National Assessment, we have to examine why making an 'assessment' is no longer giving a child a 'score out of 10', but has to do with **making decisions**.

The 10 levels into which all knowledge and skills to be taught in schools is now arranged are established in law. The Secretary of State for Education may make periodic alterations to **what** is included **within** the 10 levels but the 10 levels themselves stay put.

Assessment means making a decision within each subject area and each Attainment Target attempted as to **where** any child **is**. This is 'summative' information about the child.

## *Levels are about knowing 'where'...*

This kind of decision-making is like the kind we use in sports such as tennis or football to decide who plays whom **next**. Eventually, at Wimbledon or at Wembley only two players or teams will face each other. We get an instant assessment answer if we ask at any stage '**Where** is West Ham United?' or '**Where** is Billy Jean King?'. The answer comes as 'They've reached the semi-finals' or 'They've reached the quarter-finals'. This information tells us 'how they are doing' or their current **Level of Attainment**. The reason we know instantly 'how they are doing' is due to the fact that **we know in advance** that there are levels that we call 'finals, semi-finals..' etc.

This information is different from knowing how many goals a particular team has scored. Let's imagine West Ham United are playing Leeds United in a quarter-final match. West Ham could beat Leeds by 5, 10, 23 or 506 goals to 2! But none of these 'scores' can catapult West Ham from the quarter-final to the final. We take simply who beats whom to **decide** who goes into the next stage of the tournament.

Likewise in the National Curriculum, the levels are pre-arranged. Here, though, the child's 'opponent' is an activity which he 'plays'. If he 'beats' the activity (and perhaps a specified number of others like it) he may proceed on to challenges at the next level. If the activity defeats him, then he stays at that level and continues to work on activities and tasks at that level.

What teachers have to do is **decide** when a child has mastered skills at a certain level within any Attainment Target and then **decide** what happens to that child next.

## Multi-level activities...

Many activities which children do will be 'multi-level'. In the primary school with children in the first key stage there will be many activities that give opportunities for demonstrating skills that occur between Levels 1 and 3.

Assessment is interested in those moments when one decides that a child has now **crossed** a level **boundary**.

For each of the 10 levels within each Attainment Target, we know in advance which skills constitute attainment or mastery by the child. These are recorded in the **Statements of Attainment**. For a single-level activity it is a case of children 'beat' it, or it 'beats' them. For a multi-level activity it is a case of children possibly beating it at Level 1, the activity beating them at Level 3, children and activity 'drawing' at Level 2!

The 'who-beats-whom' will be decided by reference to those standard criteria which we call Statements of Attainment.

## So, a SAT is...?

The Statements of Attainment define the boundaries of the levels. **Once calibrated against the 10 levels, any class activity is a potential assessment task.** A SAT is simply a set of such activities. The only difference is, that **all** schools will be using activities from a limited bank of such activities which have been standardized.

All of us already know something about SATs. We all know that Attainment Targets are divided into 10 levels. This is **not** primarily a fact about curriculum content. It is a fact about assessment. Like all classroom activities and tasks in future, SATs will conform to this basic fact about a curriculum arranged in 10 levels.

### a) From 5 to 16

Children at 7 (or thereabouts) will have three SATs administered to them in the classroom. At 11 years, four SATs are being recommended. Thereafter SATs will approximate very closely to traditional subject boundaries.

### b) SATs and classwork

SATs are supposed to be indistinguishable from classwork, provided classwork during the key stage has had significant cross-curricula activities. Current SAT development policy is for cross-curriculum tasks. It is expected that SATs for the 14 year-olds will be subject-based.

SATs should not require any apparatus not commonly available in the ordinary classroom.

### c) How long will they take?

The SATs could arrive in a brown paper envelope or they could arrive in a lorry! Most of the money spent on SATs has gone into research and design. Cross-curriculum SATs will inevitably involve using substantial classroom facilities. Everything from computer-discs to children's observation schedules may come into play during a SAT.

Anything a SAT requires that cannot be expected to be found in the classroom will have to be provided within the SAT.

Some SATs may take a week to administer in the classroom, others might take three weeks.

The original specifications for the design of SATs from SEAC give freedom of interpretation, within limits, to the agencies that are designing them. After several cohorts of children have gone through the first Key Reporting Stage SATs will become more uniform in such variables as the length of time they take and so on.

## Teacher assessment

Many decisions about children in the future will be made on the basis of statutory assessment. If we rely entirely on assessments which take place every few years we run enormous risks of error.

The ambition of ERA to achieve the 'formative' uses of assessment as described in this book, is entirely without foundation if continuous assessment were to be abandoned. SATs will be formative **only when used in conjunction with continuous assessment**.

Teachers have to make judgements on a **daily** and **weekly** basis as to whether or not Sam, Shaheed or Sara should now move on to activities which involve them in learning new skills - the teacher being confident that they have sufficient competence to begin to tackle such tasks.

In the flux of daily classroom life we are often surprised that Sarah or Shaheed fail to negotiate a new problem we thought they were ready for. We can be equally surprised that they manage to do something we expected would be too difficult for them. Teaching will, and should, always retain this uncertainty. School work should never settle into an automatic, formalized pattern where we never recognize what children are capable of because we never give them opportunities to act outside formal expectations.

Continuous recording on a minute-by-minute basis would be nonsensical since teachers are continually learning about their children as they begin to relate to a new task.

## Built-in progress review times...

The National Curriculum has built-in points where we might reasonably stop and consider children's progress. The first is at the completion of substantial activities. The second is after arriving at the end of a topic, or a half-term's work. The latter period is one that we have recommended teachers in primary schools to adopt during the transition phase of moving into the National Curriculum framework.

For a period such as a half-term we can set up objectives **based on** those for the key stage for which we are in whole or part responsible. A review point at the end of a half-term can help us clarify how children have performed on activities **and also** how they have done in relation to the broader educational objectives for the half-term or term.

Continuous assessment will place the ownership of the assessment processes more in the hands of class teachers. They have a clearer understanding of the means by which they, in particular, move from the 'uncertainties' within the daily flux of teaching to the points at which decisions have been made about a child and duly recorded.

## Relation to SATs

SATs are intimately related to continuous assessment. During continuous assessment teachers will build up **estimates** of where each child is on the 10 levels within each of the Attainment Targets which have been tackled. The SAT, being a series of **standardized** tasks, helps you discover whether you have been over- or under-estimating.

In order that the SAT may do this the type of **evidence** you look for, and the way in which you **decide** on which level Sarah is in AT 6 science, must be uniform in both SAT and continuous assessment. So, SATs are not the places where one makes **most** assessment decisions about children. Most decisions should be made throughout the duration of any key stage.

**But** SATs must dictate **how** the assessment is to be carried out in **both** SATs and continuous assessment. SATs are required to adjust a teachers' best estimates in line with national estimates and they need to work for every classroom in the country.

Eventually, continuous assessment recording will be standardized. During the years of transition schools will be developing their own means and modes of operating National Assessment. Advice will be given by NCC and SEAC.

### How to organize and prepare for continuous assessment

Teachers are going to need to be more conscious of the decisions they make as a normal part of routine practice. As a corollary of this increased awareness, they will need to write down and record many more things and in much greater detail than was necessary previously. Good preparation for continuous assessment will include the following:

❑ Producing a written plan for a term, or a half-term's work for the class, along with some means of recording the Attainment Targets and levels which have been focussed upon.

❑ Recording as many of the activities which each child does in each week as possible. It is helpful if a good number of these activities are themselves calibrated. Or if you can note your own feelings as to which skills the activities involved and therefore to which Attainment Targets/Levels they apply. (See section on Task Analysis page 66.)

❑ Keeping a more general record of the activities and tasks a child does which are less closely monitored and which are a part of the routine management of the class. These might include such things as playing in the 'Home Corner', tidying the classroom, playing in the sand-pit, answering the telephone, showing visitors around the school and so on. Eventually, such parts of children's time may also become part of an assessment record. Answering the telephone, for example, uses skills specified in English, AT 1. Playing in the sand-pit uses skills specified in maths AT 8.

❑ Describing a child's work in terms of which levels they are achieving. Through an amalgamation of your own experience, and an increasing familiarity with the criteria pertaining to each level, you will begin to internalize the knowledge as to the level at which a pupil is operating. This will then need to be recorded.

## Sample National Curriculum record-keeping

NATIONAL CURRICULUM

NAME...................................................................................

| | Level 1<br>a b c d | Level 2<br>a b c d e f g h | Level 3<br>a b c d e f g h i |
|---|---|---|---|
| **Science** | | | |
| 1 Exploration | ☐ ☐ | ☐ ☐ ☐ ☐ ☐ | ☐ ☐ ☐ ☐ ☐ ☐ ☐ ☐ |
| 2 Variety of Life | ☐ | ☐ ☐ | ☐ ☐ ☐ |
| 3 Processes of Life | ☐ | ☐ ☐ ☐ | |
| 4 Genetics/Evolution | ☐ | ☐ | ☐ |
| 5 Human influences | ☐ | ☐ ☐ | ☐ ☐ |
| 6 Materials | ☐ | ☐ ☐ ☐ | ☐ ☐ |
| 9 The Earth | ☐ ☐ | ☐ ☐ ☐ ☐ | ☐ ☐ ☐ ☐ ☐ |
| 10 Forces | ☐ | ☐ | ☐ ☐ |
| 11 Electric/magnets | ☐ | ☐ ☐ | ☐ ☐ |
| 12 Information technology | ☐ | ☐ ☐ | ☐ ☐ ☐ |
| 13 Energy | ☐ ☐ | ☐ ☐ | ☐ ☐ ☐ |
| 14 Sound and music | ☐ | ☐ ☐ | ☐ ☐ |
| 15 Light | ☐ ☐ | ☐ ☐ | ☐ ☐ |
| 16 Earth in Space | ☐ ☐ ☐ | ☐ ☐ ☐ ☐ | ☐ ☐ |
| **Maths** | | | |
| 1 Use of Maths | ☐ ☐ ☐ | ☐ ☐ ☐ | ☐ ☐ ☐ |
| 2 Number | ☐ ☐ | ☐ ☐ | ☐ ☐ ☐ |
| 3 Number | ☐ | ☐ ☐ ☐ | ☐ ☐ ☐ |
| 4 Number | ☐ | ☐ | ☐ ☐ |
| 5 Number | ☐ | ☐ ☐ | ☐ ☐ ☐ |
| 6 Algebra | | ☐ | ☐ |
| 8 Measuring | ☐ | ☐ ☐ ☐ | ☐ ☐ ☐ |
| 9 Use of Maths | ☐ ☐ ☐ | ☐ ☐ ☐ | ☐ ☐ ☐ |
| 10 Shape | ☐ ☐ | ☐ ☐ | ☐ |
| 11 Shape | ☐ ☐ | ☐ ☐ | ☐ ☐ |
| 12 Handling Data | ☐ | ☐ ☐ ☐ | ☐ ☐ |
| 13 Handling Data | ☐ ☐ | ☐ ☐ | ☐ ☐ |
| 14 Handling Data | ☐ | ☐ | ☐ ☐ ☐ |
| **Language** | | | |
| 1 Speaking/Listening | ☐ ☐ ☐ | ☐ ☐ ☐ ☐ | ☐ ☐ ☐ ☐ |
| 2 Reading | ☐ ☐ ☐ ☐ | ☐ ☐ ☐ ☐ ☐ ☐ | ☐ ☐ ☐ ☐ ☐ ☐ |
| 3 Writing | ☐ | ☐ ☐ ☐ ☐ | ☐ ☐ ☐ ☐ |
| 4 Spelling | ☐ ☐ ☐ | ☐ ☐ ☐ ☐ | ☐ ☐ ☐ ☐ |
| 5 Handwriting | ☐ | ☐ ☐ | ☐ |

**Fig. 3.1**

### How to record plans

The first stage in appropriate National Curriculum record-keeping involves recording the teacher's plan. This does not involve every single child's individual scheme of work in detail. But it does mean keeping two records:

**a)** A list of the main activities and tasks outlined in the plan, together with their calibrations. This means that we know which skills in which Statements of Attainment in which Attainment Targets the activities involve.

**b)** A simple chart of which subjects, Attainment Targets and levels are being covered by the teacher in this term's or half-term's plan.

Both these records really form a part of the planning process. Neither are complicated or time-consuming to keep, although they rely upon the work that has gone into the teacher's planning itself. Detailed examples of both types of record are given in Chapter Four under the heading of 'Planning a Scheme of Work'.

### How to record the maths, science, English, etc. done by each child

We want to keep a record of all the work done by each child under the National Curriculum Statement of Attainment headings. Then we can consult this record to see:

**i)** what Attainment Targets in which subjects a particular child has been working in;

**ii)** at what level, approximately, the child seems to be working in each of those Attainment Targets.

| Class 6 | Recognize simple shapes | Count up to 20 | Count up to 100 | |
|---------|-------------------------|----------------|-----------------|---|
| Fred    |                         |                |                 | |
| Annie   |                         |                |                 | |
| Harry   |                         |                |                 | |
| Wilf    |                         |                |                 | |
| Hilda   |                         |                |                 | |

**Fig. 3.2**

This record is very much the teacher's own. It is not a printed or dupli-cated common form, but rather it is a chart which teachers draw up themselves. Using a large piece of paper they create a grid.

The row headings are the children's names.

The column headings are the parts of each Statement of Attainment that a teacher knows the children will be having some experience in for the period to which this chart applies, usually a half-term.

It is important that teachers split up each Statement of Attainment themselves into the skills they think are separable. For example, one infant teacher might split AT2 Level 1 in maths into:

| Class 6 Records Day-to-day | Count numbers up to 10 | Read and write numbers to 10 | Order numbers to 10 | Understand that the size of the set is given by last number | Understand conservation of number |
|---|---|---|---|---|---|
| Fred | | | | | |
| Annie | | | | | |

Fig. 3.3

Another teacher might split it into:

| Class 6 Records Day-to-day | Count and order numbers to 10 | Read numbers to 10 | Write numbers to 10 | Conservation & last number in a set = size of set | |
|---|---|---|---|---|---|
| Fred | | | | | |
| Annie | | | | | |

Fig. 3.4

## Methods of keeping the chart up-to-date...

At the end of each day, you take out the chart and go along each child's line in turn putting a dot in every box where you feel he or she has had some experience that day.

| | Count to 10 | Order Nos. to 10 | Count 10-20 | Order Nos. 10-20 | Read Nos. to 10 | Read Nos. to 10 |
|---|---|---|---|---|---|---|
| Fred | | | ■ | ■ | | ■ |
| Annie | ■ | ■ | | | | |
| Harry | ■ | ■ | | | ■ | |
| Wilf | ■ | | | | ■ | |
| Hilda | | | | | | |

**Fig. 3.5**

The dots do **not** say that the teacher thinks that Harry or Jane has understood or completed satisfactorily work under that heading. The dot does **not** say that they have acquired that skill. It simply records their experiences of an activity or task which will (hopefully) lead to their acquiring that skill.

❑ Some activities will allow the teacher to put dots in several boxes. The coin sort on page 46 will involve the child doing work under the following headings:
  Maths AT1, Level 1, AT2, Levels 1 or 2
  AT3, Levels 1 or 2, AT8, Level 1
❑ Some children will need to have 18 dots in a particular box before the teacher is confident that further work under that heading would be inappropriate and they are ready to move on to the next level. Other children may only need one or two dots before this stage is reached.
❑ This method of recording will allow you to keep a formal record of all the incidental maths, English or science that they do. As mentioned earlier, not all activities are pre-planned or written down.

# The Coin Sorting Machine

Try and find the coins to put in the top of the sorting machine.

Now put them in the sorting machine, but BE CAREFUL!

Look carefully and make sure each coin follows the right route.

You should finish with one coin in each box.

Rub over the coins with a crayon.

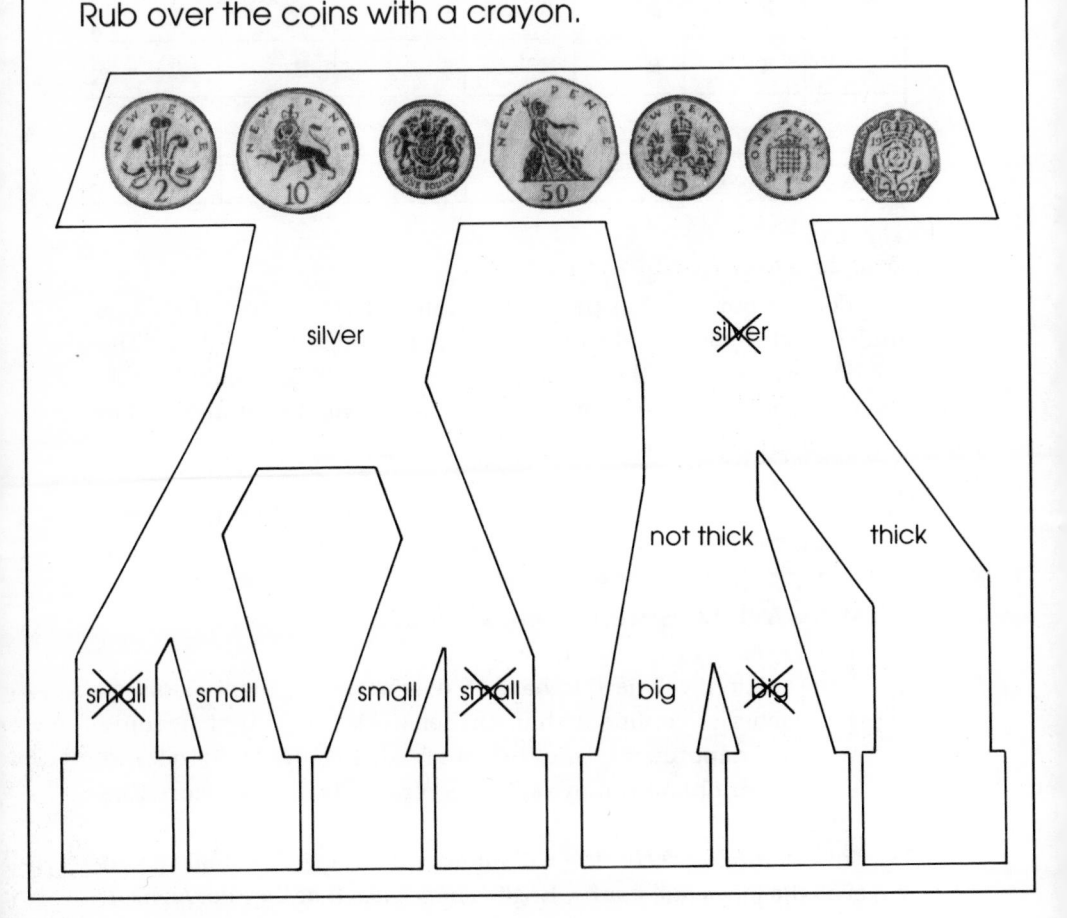

**Fig 3.6**

You often get a child, or the whole class to do a piece of maths incidentally, as when you tell the children in PE to see how many times they can hop without putting a foot to the floor. For infants, there is an important counting aspect to this activity. The dot chart allows you to put a dot in the relevant boxes (maths AT2, Level 1 in this case) by each child's name. It thus allows you to keep a record of **all** the maths, English, etc. which the child does, and **not** just the pre-planned part.

This chart provides a quick and easy means of:

❏ looking along a particular child's row and ascertaining at what levels in each Profile Component he or she is mostly working. This is very useful in terms of reporting back to parents.
❏ looking at the chart as a whole to help you realize which areas of your plan in terms of Attainment Targets you are covering and which you have not yet reached.

## How to keep individual child records

Every teacher and school will continue to keep detailed records on each child. Some LEAs have a format for these. For example, the ILEA produced an excellent language record. These individual records should involve a parent perspective, and with older children, a pupil perspective as well. The work of RANSAC shows clearly that such records should:

❏ concentrate on positive achievement;
❏ involve both the parents and the pupil.

In terms of National Curriculum record-keeping, it is important that such records include the necessary information as to where the child is, in terms of level, on each Attainment Target.

## Targeting particular Statements of Attainment

To keep individual records on each child it is very helpful if you can plan into normal classroom work a set of activities which target particular Statements of Attainment. You can then observe a specific child or group of children closely as they do these activities. You are then in a good position to make a judgement about what level each child has reached in those Attainment Targets.

This system of record-keeping is referred to again in Chapters Four and Five, where we provide a detailed example of classroom practice with reference to an imaginary teacher's topic, planning and delivery of the curriculum.

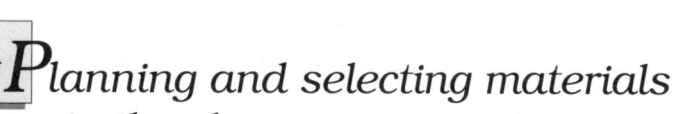

CHAPTER FOUR

# *P*lanning and selecting materials in the classroom

It is clear from the previous two chapters that the National Curriculum will mean major changes in how teachers work and, for some, the ways in which they organize their time. We must now plan our curriculum in such a way that we can provide the following:

1  A series of classroom activities, tasks and resources which will enable the children to cover the curriculum content outlined in a number of selected Attainment Targets across the core and foundation subjects.
2  A means of ensuring that each child is able to work at a level commensurate with their needs and attainments.
3  A method by which, over the course of a key stage, a sufficiently broad curriculum has been covered, including most of the Attainment Targets in the core and foundation subjects.

We saw in Chapter Two how the whole framework of the National Curriculum is based on **assessment**. Teaching itself is now one part of that framework. It is true that ERA does not tell us **how** to teach. It does not directly prescribe particular forms of classroom organization or ways of teaching. But teachers will have to organize their classrooms and teach in ways which enable them to deliver the National Curriculum entitlement to each child. This delivery begins with a scheme of work.

## How to produce a scheme of work

The scheme of work supplies the connection between the Programmes of Study and each child's assessment profile. The scheme of work must apply to **individual** children. It cannot be envisaged as a global class-room plan or as a 'splash diagram' of the class topic for that term.

In order to fulfill the function prescribed for it in the National Curriculum, the scheme of work must be part of that process, outlined in Chapter Two, in which we obtain formative criteria for the development of each child's next syllabus.

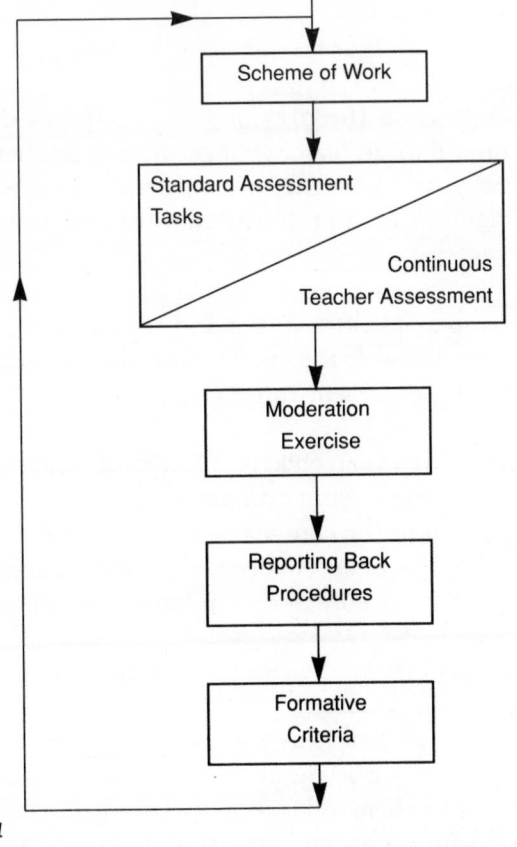

**Fig. 4.1**

Each child's assessment profile will be unique and so, in order to ensure that the formative purpose of assessment is served, children will require their own scheme of work tailor-made to their specific strengths and weaknesses.

The second thing to be aware of is that drawing up a scheme of work within the framework of the National Curriculum entails familiarity with the relevant Programmes of Study and Statements of Attainment for the relevant key stage.

A process by which you can produce an individual scheme of work for each child in your class can be broken down into six stages:

**How to produce a scheme of work**

```
┌─────────────────────────────┐
│ 1   Consider the children's │
│     levels of operation.    │
└─────────────────────────────┘
              │
              ▼
┌─────────────────────────────┐
│ 2   Choose a topic.         │
└─────────────────────────────┘
              │
              ▼
┌─────────────────────────────┐
│ 3   Consult Programmes      │
│     of Study and            │
│     Attainment Targets.     │
└─────────────────────────────┘
              │
              ▼
┌─────────────────────────────┐
│ 4   Select materials.       │
└─────────────────────────────┘
              │
              ▼
┌─────────────────────────────┐
│ 5   Plan and list all the   │
│ activities, tasks, worksheets, │
│ etc. for first 2/3 weeks.   │
└─────────────────────────────┘
              │
              ▼
┌─────────────────────────────┐
│ 6   Plot individual routes  │
│     through plan.           │
└─────────────────────────────┘
```

*Fig. 4.2*

It should be noted that detailed schemes of work will be drawn up frequently within any key stage. In the primary school, and particularly for infant teachers, this may involve planning as often as twice termly. In the secondary school it might sometimes be possible to plan a whole year's work in detail.

We are now going to follow this six-step process. At certain points, we shall illustrate this process using a worked example and discussing each step in some detail. The imagined class consists of a mixed Yr5/Yr6 group and the teacher's chosen topic is 'Aliens'.

## 1 How to consider the assessment status, the 'level' of the children

You will need to have an overall picture of the levels of work which will be appropriate for the children in your class. You will need to consider both the class as a whole in relation to the Programme of Study for the age range of children and also the Attainment Levels of the particular children in that class.

Since National Curriculum content is arranged in 10 Levels of Achievement, every piece of work the child does can be used as a reference to a level on one or more Attainment Targets. So it is essential that you have an idea at which level children are operating in a particular curriculum area in order to set them appropriate work. Conversely, by recording which activities and tasks children have done we can start to get an idea of the levels at which they are operating. Although children will not work at the same level all the time, we can obtain nonetheless, if the context is taken into account, a **partial** assessment profile. It is then possible to ensure that each child is progressing.

As a teacher, you may or may not have access to information about the children's Levels of Attainment which will help. We can consider two cases:

### a) Children starting school

If you are dealing with a reception class, there will be a particular problem in that no assessment information will necessarily be available. You will then have to provide a variety of activities where the level at which the activity is done depends on how the child performs. In practice this is little different from what is currently done in the reception class.

## b) Children of 7, 11 and 14

If you have children who have just progressed from one key stage to another, you will have a great deal of quite detailed information about each child's achievement in each Profile Component. This information will be very helpful in drawing up schemes of work, although you will also need to check this information against your experience of the children themselves as they start working with you. A summer holiday can make a lot of difference, and a child who was assessed as Level 2 in Number and Measures in April, may by September be operating comfortably at Level 3 or even 4.

In general, teachers will have access to a great deal more detailed information about the levels at which children are operating. However, it is important to bear in mind two points:

i)   The levels on the National Curriculum are very broad. You will still need to ascertain which **specific** skills children have and where they need practice. This is discovered as you work with the children in your class and cannot be predicted in advance.

ii)  Much other information about individual children is as relevant and important as it always was. This includes such things as children's behaviour, their patterns of working, concentration span, relation to peers, etc. It remains vital that you consider all this information when planning.


## 2 *How to choose a topic*

You will select a topic or a set of topics to study during the next term or half term. In the primary school this may be cross-curricular, or it may be subject based. In the secondary school it will probably be in one subject area.

The subject working groups and the NCC recommend that teachers seriously consider a cross-curricular approach for at least some part of their classroom time. It is a good strategy to enable you to cover all the foundation subjects required under the National Curriculum. It is not practical to cover three core subjects and seven foundation subjects consecutively.

It will be necessary to approach some of these in parallel through an integrated approach. In any case the teacher needs to be able to say which Attainment Targets each child is covering and at what levels.

## Example - Topic ALIENS

For this example we have concentrated upon the core subjects, maths, science and English. This topic is worked out simply as a guide to the **processes** involved in drawing up a scheme of work and is **not** intended as the only model.

The activities in this topic will include those which involve one subject only and those which include work in more than one subject area. For example, describing the alien's home planet or star will involve some science and some English. Making extra-terrestrial invaders, using the book by Michael Grater, will include some science, some maths and some art/craft. On the other hand, communicating with the aliens, talking about language and the functions words serve and so on, will involve activities which are catagorized under the heading of English.

The topic as outlined above draws upon the following references:

**Grinny** - by Nicholas Fisk (Puffin)
This book concerns a boy who is visited by an alien masquerading as his great aunt. She can hypnotize adults so that they believe her but children can escape. They develop a means of talking to her which involves looking just to the right of her eyes called 'eyes right'. Electricity upsets this alien. The book, which is very exciting, will be read out loud and will be used to generate work on electricity and communication.

**Dr Who and the Daleks** - by David Whittaker (Armada)
This concerns life forms (Daleks) which have evolved in different conditions. The Daleks harness static electricity in order to move around. The book will be used to stimulate work on the evolution of life and electricity and magnetism.

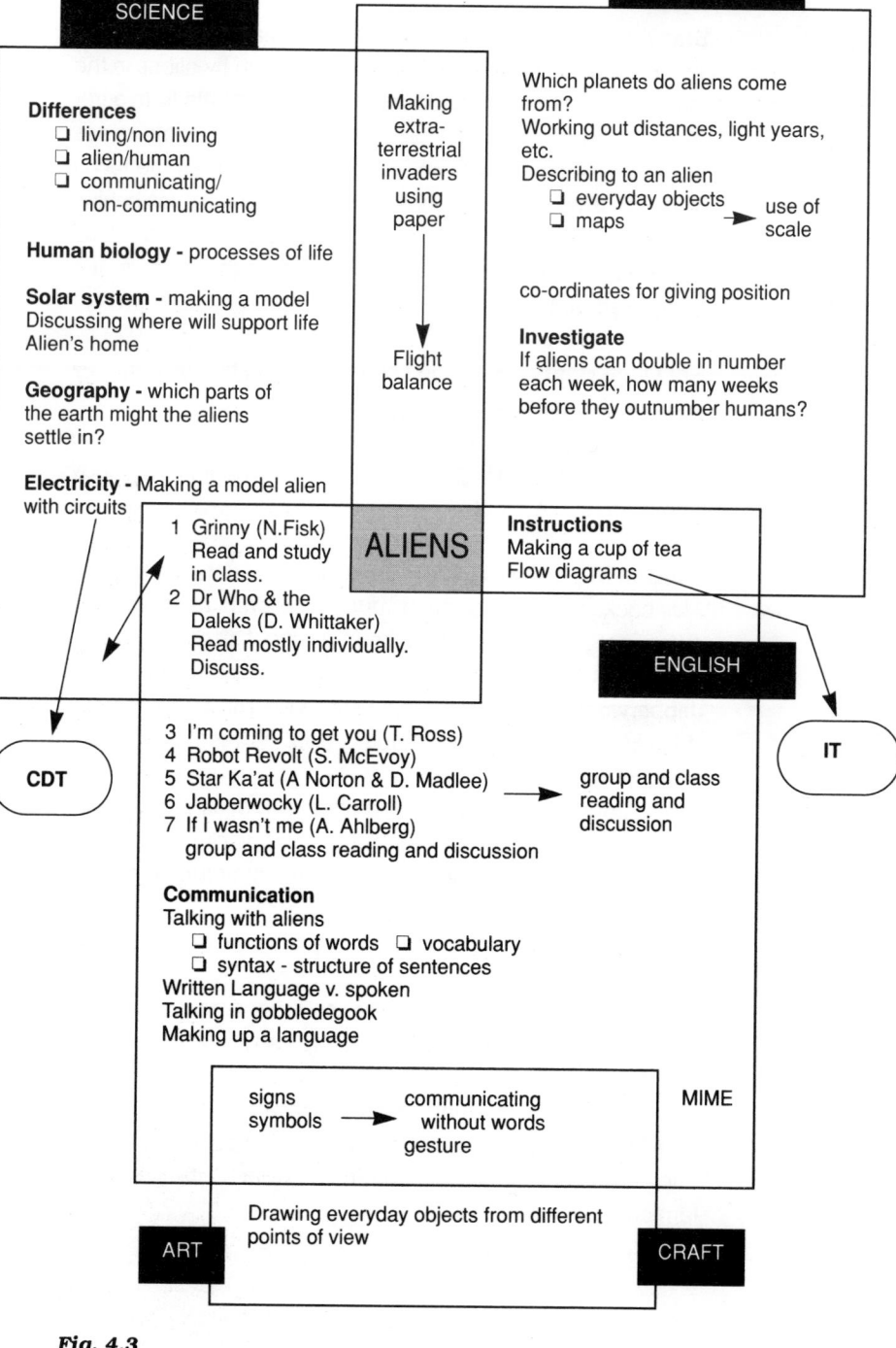

**SCIENCE**

**Differences**
- ❏ living/non living
- ❏ alien/human
- ❏ communicating/ non-communicating

**Human biology -** processes of life

**Solar system -** making a model
Discussing where will support life
Alien's home

**Geography -** which parts of the earth might the aliens settle in?

**Electricity -** Making a model alien with circuits

Making extra-terrestrial invaders using paper

↓

Flight balance

**MATHS**

Which planets do aliens come from?
Working out distances, light years, etc.
Describing to an alien
- ❏ everyday objects
- ❏ maps → use of scale

co-ordinates for giving position

**Investigate**
If aliens can double in number each week, how many weeks before they outnumber humans?

1 Grinny (N.Fisk)
  Read and study in class.
2 Dr Who & the Daleks (D. Whittaker)
  Read mostly individually.
  Discuss.

**ALIENS**

**Instructions**
Making a cup of tea
Flow diagrams

**ENGLISH**

**CDT**

3 I'm coming to get you (T. Ross)
4 Robot Revolt (S. McEvoy)
5 Star Ka'at (A Norton & D. Madlee)
6 Jabberwocky (L. Carroll)
7 If I wasn't me (A. Ahlberg)
  group and class reading and discussion

→ group and class reading and discussion

**IT**

**Communication**
Talking with aliens
- ❏ functions of words  ❏ vocabulary
- ❏ syntax - structure of sentences
Written Language v. spoken
Talking in gobbledegook
Making up a language

signs
symbols → communicating without words gesture

MIME

Drawing everyday objects from different points of view

ART

CRAFT

*Fig. 4.3*

**Star Ka'at** - by Andre Norton & Dorothy Madlee (Blackie)
This book also concerns the visitation of earth by aliens in the form of strange cats - a super intelligent race of cats from outer space who have come to save earth. The book again raises the issue of communication. It will also be used as the focus of a discussion on appearance and reality and what lies behind the image of 'ordinariness'. The book is quite easy and will be partly read out loud in class by the children themselves and partly read at home.

**Not Quite Human, Batteries Not Included** - by Seth McEvoy (Collins, Dragon Grafton)
This book is popular among children of this age and can be used as private reading. It starts a whole series about a boy who is, in fact, a robot.

**I'm Coming to Get You** - by Tony Ross (Andersen Press)
This book, intended for much younger children, deals with the surprise visit of an alien and the relativity of size.

**Jabberwocky** - by Lewis Carrol from 'I Like This Poem' (Puffin)
**If I wasn't me** - by Alan Ahlberg from 'Please Mrs Butler' (Puffin)
These poems will be used to explore the ideas surrounding communication of the self to others. Jabberwocky will be used to start the work in English on words and their functions.

**Extraterrestrial Invaders that Fly** - by Michael Grater (Cut and Fold Books, Dover)
This book gives some excellent ideas in paper folding and will be used to start off the maths on shape and space.

**Galactic Aliens** - by Alan Frank (Chartwell Books)
**The Road to the Stars** - by Iain Nicolson (Westbridge Books)
These two books assist and inform the work on the solar system and the galaxy.

## 3 How to consult the Programmes of Study and Attainment Targets

The next stage in the production of a scheme of work is the careful study of the Attainment Targets within the appropriate range of levels. Details of which Attainment Targets children are covering and at what levels, form part of the information required under ERA. This means that teachers need to keep a record of which parts of the Programmes of Study they are attempting to deliver in any one term or half term. They also need to record the Attainment Targets and their levels. The mechanisms for doing this with reference to individual children, were discussed in detail in Chapter Three.

### Example - topic ALIENS

The topic will include work in the following parts of the Programmes of Study:

**Science**
❏ Exploration of science;
promoting the raising and answering of questions;
exploring with increasing precision;
building on existing practical skills;
involving variables to be controlled in a 'fair test';
encouraging the formulation of testable hypotheses;
using equipment and measurement;
involving problems to be solved qualitatively but with some move towards quantative solutions.
❏ Knowledge and understanding of science particularly those parts which relate to the investigation and measurement of similarities and differences between different life forms.
Also those parts relating to forces and energy and electricity and the making of circuits.
Finally, some work will be done in the area of the Earth in space.

**Maths**
❏ Using and applying mathematics;
❏ Number, especially dealing with large numbers, addition and subtraction and estimation;

❏ Algebra, especially those concerned with doubling;
❏ Measures, understanding the relationship between units, making sensible estimates;
❏ Shape and space, constructing 2 and 3D shapes; specifying location by means of co-ordinates; recognizing symmetry.

### English
❏ Speaking and listening in a variety of situations including discussion in groups, and as a whole class. The children will have to formulate and make responses and will be particularly involved in giving and receiving instructions.
❏ Reading: the children will be read to, will read aloud and will read silently. They will have ample opportunity to discuss what they read since some of the books are intended to be read by everyone. The children will be encouraged to continue their reading at home. The children will also be working on the use of signs and symbols to convey meaning.
❏ Writing: the children will write in a number of different styles and contexts on this topic. It will be necessary to observe the purposes of a variety of sorts of writing and also to study the functions of different parts of speech.

Once a topic has been chosen, you can then consider the **specific skills** and knowledge that you want the children to acquire throughout that term's work. This is to pose the question, 'Precisely what do I want the children to learn?', or put round the other way, 'What do I intend to teach the children this term?'. To decide this, you consult the subject documents of the National Curriculum.

It is expected that teachers will rapidly achieve a familiarity with the precise details of the Attainment Targets in each subject they are required to teach, and the relevant parts of the Programmes of Study. In the primary school, where teachers are rarely subject-based, this means that teachers do have to retain a considerable quantity of information in order to be able to plan their curriculum. To assist this process we have developed a means of recording the teachers' plans with reference to the precise Attainment Targets and parts of the Programmes of Study. (See pages 116/117)

The teacher studies a chart on which **all** the Statements of Attainment at the appropriate levels are laid out. In maths, these are substantially the same as the Programmes of Study. In English and science this chart needs to be cross-referenced to another table showing the Programmes of Study. Since all the Attainment Targets are on one piece of paper it is possible to record using a system of dots which parts are being addressed in this term's or half-term's work.

## Example - Topic ALIENS

In this topic the teacher has planned a number of activities and pieces of work which fall under various headings supplied by the Statements of Attainment:

| SCIENCE | | |
|---|---|---|
| AT 1 | 4 | 1, 2, 3, 5, 6, 8, 10 |
|  | 5 | 3 |
| AT 2 | 4 | 1, 2, 3 |
|  | 5 | 1, 4 |
| AT 3 | 4 | 1, 2 |
| AT 4 | 4 |  |
|  | 5 |  |
| AT 10 | 4 | 1, 2, 3, 4 |
|  | 5 | 4 |
| AT 11 | 3 | 1, 2 |
|  | 4 |  |
|  | 5 | 1, 2 |
|  | 6 | 1 |
| AT 12 | 3 | 1, 2 |
|  | 4 | 1, |
| AT 13 | 3 | 1, 3 |
|  | 4 | 1, 2 |
| AT 16 | 4 | 1, 2, 3 |
|  | 5 | 1 |

**Fig. 4.5 (i)**

| ENGLISH | | |
|---|---|---|
| AT 1 | 3 upwards ↓ | 1, 2, 3, 4 |
| AT 2 | 3 upwards ↓ | 1, 2, 3, 5 |
| AT 3 | 3 upwards ↓ | 1, 2, 3, 5 |
| AT 4 | 3 upwards ↓ | 1, 3 |
| AT 5 | 3 upwards ↓ | |

| MATHS | | |
|---|---|---|
| AT 1 | 4 | 1, 2, 3 |
| AT 2 | 4 | 1, 3 |
| AT 3 | 4 | 2, 3 |
| AT 4 | 4 | 1, 2 |
| | 5 | 1 |
| AT 5 | 4 | 1 |
| AT 7 | 4 | 1 |
| AT 8 | 3 | 1, 2, 3 |
| | 4 | 1, 2, 3 |
| | 5 | 1, 2 |
| AT 9 | 4 | 1, 2 |
| | 5 | 2 |
| AT 10 | 4 | 1, 2 |
| | 5 | 1 |
| AT 11 | 3 | 1, 2 |
| | 4 | 1, 2 |
| | 5 | 1 |

*Fig. 4.5 (ii)*

From this list teachers can record theAttainment Targets and levels covered so as to have this information in a readily accessible form. The system of recording can be up-dated as time progresses. For example, we use a 'traffic-light' code. At the beginning of the term you put a **green** dot in any section of the chart which you think your work this term will be addressing. Half way through the term you add an **orange** dot to any sections where you feel the work is continuing well and some coverage of these matters and skills has taken place. At the end of the term, you put a **red** dot in any sections where coverage has been substantially achieved.

| LEVEL | AT 1 | 2 | 3 | 4 |
|---|---|---|---|---|
| 1 |  |  | ■ |  |
| 2 | ■ | ■ | ■ | ■ |
| 3 | ■ | ■ |  |  |

*Fig. 4.6*

**Note:** This is **not** a record of any individual child's scheme of work. It is simply a record for you and those who have the children after you, of which Attainment Targets have been covered and which have not. It enables teachers to ensure that over any key stage the relevant Attainment Targets and parts of the Programmes of Study have been covered.

**It checks and describes the teacher's route through the National Curriculum map.**

## 4 How to select materials

This is the creative (and difficult!) part of the process where you decide what you hope to achieve and **how** you can hopefully succeed. Educational objectives have to be translated into classroom tasks, pieces of work and practical activities for the children to do. Experienced teachers may have a range of activities up their sleeves which enable them to cover most topics and contingencies. But most teachers will need to consult a variety of sources to find the activities, tasks and materials they need to achieve their objectives.

## a) Which materials?

It is important to realize that not all the activities and tasks that children will do in the classroom are pre-planned or designed. Particularly in the infant classroom, a reasonable percentage of the children's work is given by the teacher as the result of an instant decision. This is because good teaching is **responsive**.

A child brings the teacher a model he or she has made out of Lego. The teacher responds by admiring the model and asking the child to count the number of blocks used to make it. A teacher talking with the class on the rug may decide to use an atlas to point out the location of a particular place that has come up in the course of the conversation. If there is five minutes to spare while waiting for playtime, a teacher may do some number songs and rhymes with the class. Many activities are created on the spur of the moment in response to a particular learning situation.

As far as the advance planning of National Curriculum delivery goes there are three possible sources of materials:

### i) New calibrated materials

These are materials which have been produced or re-designed since the National Curriculum and are already calibrated against the National Curriculum. This means that they will specify on them which Attainment Targets and which levels the materials are designed to cover. It also means that the curriculum coverage of these materials is likely to be compatible with the layout of the curriculum in the subject documents.

## Example - Topic ALIENS

The teacher selects a worksheet from the IMPACT Pack of Materials (4.1), which outlines a number puzzle.

## Dr Who

Dr Who is marooned on a planet and aliens have hidden his Tardis.

They know the 2 numbers, (co-ordinates), which will give the Tardis's position.

The aliens won't tell Dr Who the numbers but they don't lie.

Dr Who thinks that he can trick the aliens into telling him the numbers.

This is Dr Who's trick:

Think of two numbers between 1 and 9, then:

| | |
|---|---|
| take the 1st number | E.g. 7 & 5 |
| x 10 | 70 |
| + 5 | 75 |
| x 10 | 750 |
| - 50 | 700 |
| + 2nd number | 705 |

Tell me your answer ...(705).

Now Dr Who can tell where the aliens have hidden his Tardis!

**Fig. 4.7**

This sheet is already calibrated against the Statements of Attainment in maths so that the teacher is told that it involves:

AT1, Level 4, AT3, Level 4, AT5, Level 5.

The teacher is then able to transcribe this information for use in keeping class records.

## ii) Existing materials

These are resources which were around before the introduction of the National Curriculum and which teachers will want to continue using. They are not calibrated with the relevant Attainment Targets and so teachers themselves will need to match these against the Statements of Attainment to obtain the necessary calibrations. This will involve an analysis of these materials in terms of the skills they involve.

### *Example - Topic ALIENS*

The teacher has decided to use an activity from a book to reinforce some of the children's number skills. The layout and context of the worksheet fits with the topic:
The worksheet is not calibrated and the teacher will have to decide which Statements of Attainment record the skills the activity requires of the children.

## iii) Teacher-designed tasks

These are activities which teachers create in order to implement a particular part of their plan. They are designed in advance, rather than being dreamt up on the spur of the moment in the classroom, but they have an aspect to them which is likely to be specifically tailored to particular children. These materials are personal rather than general in the way that commercially-produced resources have to be.

### *Example - Topic ALIENS*

The teacher asks the children to write a poem in which at least part of the language used is 'nonsense' language. The teacher reads them 'Jabberwocky' and then the children spend some time discussing the different types of words in simple sentences. The children have then to draft their poem, discuss it with the teacher and with the others in the group, redraft it, bring it back for final corrections, and then write it out.

# Monster invasion

The Earth is being invaded by monsters. These monsters are very powerful! They can double their number every hour!

If only **one** monster arrives on Earth, can you work out how many hours it will take until there are too many monsters for the number to fit on your calculator? Here is how.

Press the number  on your calculator. Then double it by pressing

Do this again. How many times can you double the number until it gets too big for the screen and an appears?

There is a quick way to make your calculator do something such as multiply by **2** again and again. Press , then and then again. With some calculators you may have to press instead.
Try it out!

How many monsters will there be after a day and a half?

**Hint**
There are **24** hours in a day.

Try to find out how many hours it would take for the number of monsters to reach **1,000,000 –** one million!

This activity is not written down anywhere, and the teacher is again required to think about the skills it requires and where they are mentioned in the Statements of Attainment.

## b) How to calibrate materials

The process of calibrating materials - i.e. providing a description for any activity that gives its 'location' on the 10 levels and its 'coverage' of Attainment Targets - is outlined in the 'task analysis' shown below:

```
How to calibrate activities

1   Study the activity. Write a list
    of the subjects (e.g. maths,
    science) you think it falls
    under.

2   Now write a list of the skills
    required to do the activity under
    each subject.

3   Consult the necessary Attainment
    Targets and Statements of
    Attainment.

4   Decide which Attainment Targets
    include the skills named.

5   Decide at what level these
    particular skills occur.

Note: It is not always necessary to
write the list of subjects or skills
if the activity is simple.
```

**Fig. 4.9**

### c) How to find resources

### i) Collaboration with colleagues

A conversation with another person can make a great deal of difference. Some schools and teachers plan in teams as a matter of course, even where teachers are not necessarily team teaching. Two or three teachers can share their knowledge of resources, and can suggest books, ideas, software and so on to each other. Discussion can generate new ideas for ways to cover a particular topic. Previous experiences can be drawn upon so that teachers teaching top infants this year can perhaps assist colleagues teaching reception by sharing some of the things they found successful when they had reception two years ago.

### ii) Teachers' Centres

This is the stage in planning where in-service training is most useful. An advisory teacher or a Teachers' Centre may be able to suggest sources for further materials or even offer a direct supply of ideas for classroom activities. In some cases actual classroom materials may be loaned or supplied.

## 5 How to list activities, etc.

We need to plan and list the activities, tasks and pieces of work to be tackled by the children - in detail for the immediate future and in outline for later on.

It is important at this stage that the differing needs of individual children are taken into account. Tasks and activities appropriate to several Levels of Achievement will need to be incorporated into the plan so that children can work at their own attainment ceiling and beyond. The corollary of this is that not every child will do each activity named. We are clearly planning for a situation in which the children will work in groups or even on their own some of the time. In this way the varying demands of children across a range of levels can be accommodated within one termly plan.

## Example - Topic ALIENS

The teacher has planned an initial list of activities in this topic which includes:

---

**Teacher's List**
Term 2. 1.1.90                                    CLASS 6a

**1** Start reading 'Grinny' (E.AT 1/2)

**2** Read 'I'm Coming to Get You.' (E.AT 1/2)

**3** Class discussion on relativity of size (M.AT 1/8/9 E.AT1)

**4** Children to draw either an object or a scene from the point of view of an elephant or a mouse (M.AT 9/10/11)

**5** Tell the story of the aliens who can double in number each week....

**6** Set up groups to discover how many weeks till aliens outnumber humans. (M.AT 2/3/4/5)

**7** Maths Worksheets (M.AT 3/5)

**8** Talk with groups about describing and identifying everyday objects - without words (mime-gesture), with words (description - word picture).

**9** Get children to draw one object - e.g. shoes, bike, teapot from three different perspectives-front elevation, side elevation plan

---

*Fig. 4.10*

The teacher's plan at this stage is **not** a scheme of work in that it applies to the whole class rather than to an individual child. It does contain lists of activities, tasks, worksheets, workcards, commercially-produced materials and so on. These apply across the range of levels to be found in that class and it is expected that any one child will do an appropriate selection of the outlined tasks and worksheets.

The plan now produced can be described as wedge-shaped.

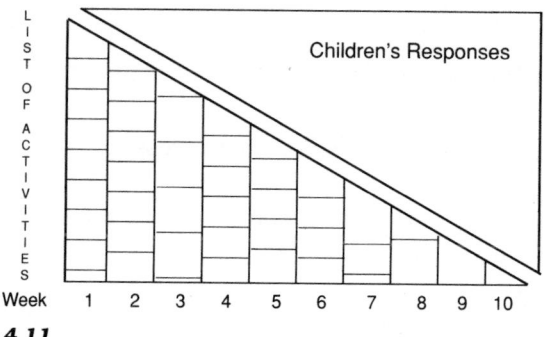 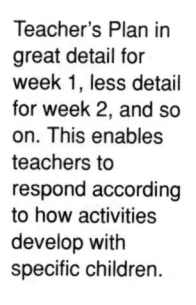

L
I
S
T

O
F

A
C
T
I
V
I
T
I
E
S

Children's Responses

Week   1   2   3   4   5   6   7   8   9   10

Teacher's Plan in great detail for week 1, less detail for week 2, and so on. This enables teachers to respond according to how activities develop with specific children.

**Fig. 4.11**

It outlines specific tasks and resources for the immediate future, gives the general direction of the work to be undertaken by the children and the teacher and specifies the Attainment Targets and levels to be covered. However, it allows for a substantial part of the work the children do to be designed or selected by the teacher **in response** to an immediate situation and having regard to the child's performance on the parts of the work already undertaken. In this way, the requirements of formativity are fulfilled.

## 6 How to plot individual routes through the plan

The final stage in the drawing up of Schemes of Work is the isolation of individual children's 'routes'. Each child will do an appropriate selection of the work planned for the whole class. The precise form this selection will take, like the plan itself, is given in some detail for the immediate future but in sufficient vagueness for some time ahead to allow for formativity and teacher response.

This means that if children progress particularly fast through one set of activities at a particular level, their route through the class-work plan can be modified to include a selection of more advanced tasks and pieces of work. Similarly, children who are experiencing difficulty in one area of the curriculum at a particular level, can continue with work at that level on those Attainment Targets until you feel they are ready to move on.

In decreasing detail as it applies to periods further removed in the future, the scheme of work is now finished. It enables teachers to supply all the information required of them by the new legislation. (See Chapter Five, page 94) for details of this.)

## Conclusion

Drawing up a scheme of work is a six-stage process:

1 Looking at the previous attainment of the children in terms of the National Curriculum levels;
2 Choosing a topic;
3 Studying the Programmes of Study and Statements of Attainment;
4 Selecting resources and materials;
5 Making a list of the activities, worksheets, tasks, books, software, etc. that the children as a whole class, will actually be doing;
6 Plotting individual routes through the plan.

These stages will involve collaborating with colleagues, studying the subject documents and taking into account the assessment information available concerning the children.

# CHAPTER FIVE

# *Delivering the National Curriculum*

## Classroom organization and curriculum delivery

There is no specific requirement under the National Curriculum for teachers to organize their classes in any particular way or teach in a particular style. However, there are certain constraints and implications:

### 1 Programmes of Study

The Subject Working Groups make recommendations in their Programmes of Study which have direct implications for methods of teaching.

### 2 Demands of Assessment

The design of assessment, either SATs or continuous teacher assessment, may lead teachers to organize their classrooms in one way rather than another.

### 3 Recommendations of NCC

The Government appointed National Curriculum Council is able to advise teachers on the best means of delivering the National Curriculum. In order to cover all the foundation subjects and to provide a 'broad and balanced' curriculum, it may be necessary to adopt one approach rather than another. The NCC is in a position to specify effective types of teaching and classroom organization.

> ○ There could be a conflict between the recommendations
> of a Subject Working Group or NCC and the demands of
> assessment in so far as classroom organization is con-
> cerned. Given the emphasis of ERA we believe that the
> demands of assessment will prove more influential.

## Modes of classroom organization

It is possible to organize the classroom in a number of different ways.
Teachers are specifically advised by the NCC to have a variety as a part
of their normal practice.

### Class teaching

The National Curriculum permits children in the same class or year
group to be at different levels. On paper at least, a child in a top junior
class could be doing work at Level 7, while other children in the same
class are working at Level 3. As we saw in the previous chapter, this
does not conflict with the idea that all children have the same curriculum entitlement.

Since different children will be expected to be at different levels, even
within an otherwise homogeneous group, it will be necessary to provide
work across a range of levels. This makes it difficult to see how teaching the whole class as a unit is possible. But note that certain
Attainment Targets **assume** that at least some of the work set will be
of this form. NCC, as well as the Subject Working Groups, recommends
that this should be so.

**For example:**
In English, AT1, Level 4, children are expected to 'speak freely and
audibly to a class'.
and in science AT1, Level 8; 'prepare and deliver a report matched to
an audience'.

Clearly it is important that some teaching in **all** stages is aimed at the
whole class and that children have the experience of responding and
initiating ideas in a large group as well as a small one.

## a) Introducing a topic

When teaching a particular topic, it is almost always helpful to introduce that topic to the class as a whole.

### Example - Topic ALIENS

Teachers set up the topic mentioning in their session the following points:

What are aliens?
  Derivation of the word - foreign, strange, outsider
  Do aliens have to be living?
  Are aliens always evil or bad?
  Do aliens have to look different?

How would we recognize an alien?
  Tests for 'human-ness'
  What are the accepted parameters for being human?

Where would an alien be likely to come from?
  Planets, (stars are too hot)
  Conditions for life

How would we communicate with an alien?
  Words, gestures, mime...

The subsequent discussion will be controlled by the teacher but as far as possible the children need to be allowed free rein in letting their imaginations suggest answers. The discussion sometimes benefits from the key points being written down in a place where everyone can see them. The children then need to follow the class discussion with some individual or group work in which the ideas expressed are consolidated and they have a chance to work out their own individual thoughts on the subject.

## b) Class activities within the topic

With a certain amount of application one activity or task can be tailored to fit the needs of pupils working at widely differing levels.

## Example - Topic Aliens

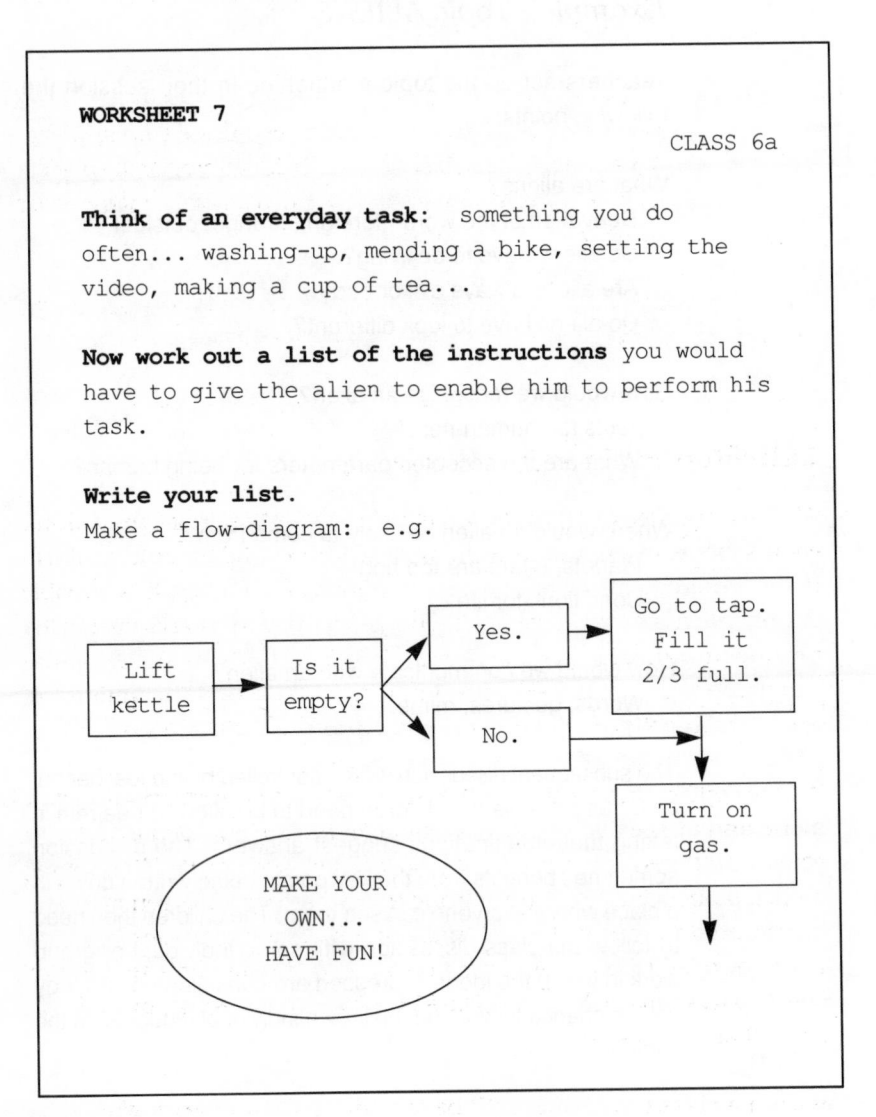

**WORKSHEET 7**

CLASS 6a

**Think of an everyday task:** something you do often... washing-up, mending a bike, setting the video, making a cup of tea...

**Now work out a list of the instructions** you would have to give the alien to enable him to perform his task.

**Write your list.**
Make a flow-diagram: e.g.

Lift kettle → Is it empty? → Yes. → Go to tap. Fill it 2/3 full.

No. → Turn on gas.

MAKE YOUR OWN... HAVE FUN!

**Fig. 5.1**

This activity can help children to:

- ❏ give precise instructions to another person; Eng AT1 (3)
- ❏ create a methodical task-plan; maths AT9 (3)
- ❏ design a flow diagram; maths AT9 (4)
- ❏ use the principal of decision trees; maths AT12 (4)
- ❏ use the computer and turn the set of instructions into a procedure. IT AT (5)

One child might take a very simple task such as making a cup of tea, another might use a more complex task such as mending a puncture on a bicycle. One child will stop at the point at which they have a simple flow diagram, another will get as far as programming a computer.

Thus one activity which could well be given to the whole class, might be done at different levels by the children themselves.

## Individualized work schemes

We have seen that within the framework of the National Curriculum, each scheme of work applied to an individual child, should conform to the requirements of formativity. We have also seen how it is possible to generate a scheme of work without having recourse to commercially-produced individualized schemes. The demands of the National Curriculum do not **necessarily** imply an increase in the amount of work which children do on their own rather than in groups.

It is accepted that there are occasions when children should work alone and at specific tasks. For example, having engaged in a group activity and been active in a joint practical task such as building a large model, doing a survey or measuring the classroom, children may well be required to record the task individually. Some activities, such as reading, need to be performed in a variety of contexts - to another child, to a group, to the whole class or school, to a teacher, to a parent, as well as to oneself.

Within a class topic, there will be specific tasks and work which the children will do on their own, often at a variety of different times.

## Example - Topic ALIENS

The teacher asks the children to do the following individual activities.

❏ write a description of the planet the aliens come from;
❏ draw a picture of the alien;
❏ draw a picture of the alien's home;
❏ work out the size of the alien, giving precise measurements.

These activities require children to use their own imagination and skills in creating their alien and his/her context.

> ### Think about it
>
> ### - The place of individual work
>
> *There will continue to be an important place for individual work, just as there will for class teaching. However, neither should dominate teaching, as they have sometimes tended to in the past. If the teacher believes that it is only what a child achieves when working alone that is important, then the children will quickly get the message that it is only individual work which 'counts', and that asking the help of others is 'cheating'. This makes a nonsense of group work.*

## Group work

The reports produced by the subject-working groups **all** suggest that group-work, children working co-operatively together, is an **essential** part of the Programmes of Study which are now included in the statutory orders. They also join TGAT in recommending that the SATs should involve group as well as individual work.

Further to this, many of the skills referred to in the Attainment Targets of all core subjects can be acquired only through group work and through children talking about what they are doing, explaining it to one another, giving and receiving information and so on. We are recommended to teach in a way which will "involve all pupils in

'chalk and talk' with teachers, as well as in individual and group work"
(5.1)

and where activities will 'involve both independent and co-operative
work'. (5.1)

## Example - Topic ALIENS

Many of the activities planned in this topic will require that the children work in groups. At a particular stage in the classwork on 'Aliens', the classroom is organized thus:

### Group A - All Y6 children
These children are making an alien. They have to build a model of him, including wiring him up using a circuit so that his heart beats and lights up. The model should be to scale.

### Group B - All Y6 children
These children are designing the alien's home on his home planet. They are considering the size of the aliens and their physical and emotional needs. They have to plan and build a scale model of this home, discussing and deciding upon suitable materials.

### Group C - All Y5 children
These children have to think about a suitable home on earth for the alien. They also must take into account his needs and size. They must plan and design this model. It does not have to be to scale, but it should incorporate some simple electric light circuitry.

### Group D - All Y5 children
These children are asked to design clothes for the alien. They must draw the clothes from different angles, clearly indicating the measurements. At a later stage, together with older children, they will design and make some miniature mock-ups of these clothes.

### Group E - Mixed Y6 and Y5 children

These children are to design a suitable car for the alien. They are to make a model of this car, which should be approximately to scale. They must discuss the materials they will need to make it, and the method of making it go.

The children are all engaged on tasks which involve them in design and technology, maths, science and art. They're working at different levels and in slightly different areas within those subjects. They will use a variety of skills in each group.

Teachers who organize their classrooms mainly around individualized work may find that they place their children at a disadvantage. Commercial schemes are affected by this too. Many teachers use these in order to have children working alone through workbooks or cards.

Working in groups enables the teacher to get some children started on one particular activity while others are finishing another task, or working individually. It also makes the use of equipment easier, since it is only necessary to have one abacus, or one set of scales or five or six calculators to have a group of children using them.

## How group work can enhance children's learning

It is not simply organizational considerations which lead us to encourage the use of group work. There is now a wealth of evidence that children's learning is enhanced by working in small groups. It is more difficult for some children - those who are quiet, obedient, and not particularly creative - to become 'invisible' or to remain unacknowledged by the teacher (5.2). It is easier for children to make friends and makes for a much healthier, more collaborative and less competitive, hierarchical structure in the class (5.3). When children have to explain something to another person, the process of explaining is itself an important step in making that knowledge or skill their own (5.4).

Allowing children to work together in groups is as close as a teacher can get to imitating the co-operative learning which happens naturally. When children become accustomed to working together in this way a number of things happen:

**i)** The children become used to having to explain things to each other and - much more difficult - having to listen to and make sense of other people's explanations.

**ii)** It has been shown in many different ways that it is not until you make a piece of knowledge or a skill **your own** in some way that you are likely to be able to remember it or transfer it to other situations. Through talking about what they have learned and particularly through 'teaching' it to others, children come to understand what they have been taught (5.5).

**iii)** Through placing the children in small groups to work, the teacher has the opportunity to exercise some control over the pattern of the social structure in a class. The teacher can enable boys to work with girls in situations where gender is becoming an increasingly divisive factor. Children who have trouble concentrating do not always have to work with the same group.

It is assumed that by group work, teachers understand that we do not envisage 'sets' i.e. a rigid structure of groups of children all at the same level. On some occasions it is helpful for children to work closely with those at the same stage in a particular subject. However, it is important that there are other situations in which children get the opportunity to work with those with quite different skills and levels of competence.

The National Curriculum states that children need to acquire specified skills, knowledge and understanding. Some of these are acquired only through working co-operatively with others in groups. Furthermore, part of the assessments will require individual children to operate successfully as part of a group. Therefore, teachers must organize their classrooms to allow children sufficient time to work collaboratively.

## Using a combination of different teaching methods

On many occasions it is possible to approach a specific part of the work planned for a particular class by including a number of teaching modes.

## Example - Topic ALIENS

In preparation for making the alien's heart pulse on the electric model, the children need to know what the average human pulse rate is, and how it is affected by certain factors such as health, exercise and age.

---

**WORKSHEET 14**

CLASS 6a

**Measure the pulse rate of** six people and record your results.

You will have to:

1   find their pulse by putting your fore-finger on their wrist.

2   count, while someone else times you 6 seconds using a stop watch.

3   write down your answer and multiply it by 10.

4   ask your victim to jump up and down 20 times (at least).

5   now repeat the pulse-taking.

---

**Fig. 5.2**

## Methods of teaching employed

### a)  Class teaching
The teacher talks to the class as a whole, setting out the problem and discussing a variety of ways of carrying out the survey.

### b) Group work

The children split into groups to carry out the survey. They are encouraged to split up different aspects of the problem, one group concentrating on a particular sort of exercise, such as pulse rate before and after jumping, and another group looking at different positions - lying, sitting, standing, upside-down, etc.

### c) Class teaching

Children are encouraged to present the results of their groups' work to the whole class. Once the results from the survey are all collected, the data is collated by the whole class, the teacher acting as 'scribe' and giving some instruction in various methods of handling this data.

### d) Individual work

The children are now asked to record the survey, using a variety of methods. They must produce written accounts, tables of figures and appropriate graphs.

### e) Group work

Working in differently composed groups, the children are asked to discuss profitable 'next lines of enquiry'. Their project is on health and they are encouraged to use the results of the pulse rate survey to point them in the direction of further study. They must discuss both the rationale and methods of their new research.

## The involvement of home

It is intended that, through the National Curriculum, parents and teachers will use the same educational vocabulary. It is crucial that parents and teachers not only speak the same language but that they also work together much more closely than has traditionally been the case. We have written elsewhere about the importance of home involvement in schools and in the curriculum (5.6). With the advent of the National Curriculum this becomes even more urgent for schools.

For the last five years we have been working on the IMPACT project which is a large research and intervention programme of structured home involvement in the curriculum. Although the results of this work are being written up and reported elsewhere, there are distinct advantages for National Curriculum delivery here which are worth a mention in this context.

The idea of a partnership between teachers and parents for the delivery of the curriculum arose from the initiatives in the late 70s and early 80s in which parents were involved in their children's learning to read. This involvement took the form of a shared-reading programme together with a structured dialogue between parents and teachers. The results of this intervention were sufficiently impressive to make a number of educationalists reconsider the traditional assumptions concerning the role of parents in their children's schooling. (5.7)

## How to involve parents in reading

Many schools now operate a shared-reading scheme of some description. This will involve the child taking home a book to share with a parent/sibling. It will also incorporate some system whereby comments on how the child is progressing are written and read by both the teacher and the parent. Some schools use a diary in which both the parent and the teacher - and in some cases the child - write daily or as frequently as possible. Other mechanisms include comment sheets or cards on which boxes are ticked or symbols employed to indicate how each day's reading went.

**Fig. 5.3**

## How to involve parents in maths - *IMPACT*

IMPACT was set up five years ago intending to mirror the shared-reading initiatives. It employs a process in which children take home weekly or fortnightly maths activities to share with a parent or sibling. The products of these activities feed back into and help construct the subsequent week's class work.

**HOW MUCH IS YOUR HAND WORTH?**

Draw around your hand.

Use a 1p coin and draw around it so that you cover your hand.

Count up your coins.

How much is your hand worth?

Try not to leave big gaps between the coins.

If you have got time try some of these:
Use a different coin.

Use a grown up's hand.

Is your hand worth more than 50p?

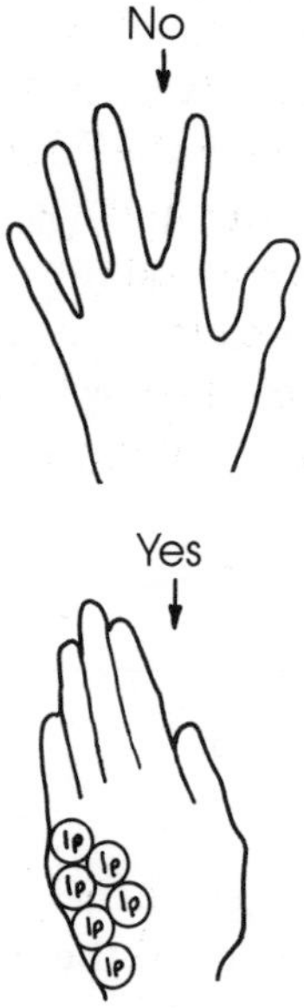

No

Yes

*Fig 5.4*

When children have drawn round their hand at home they can draw round a foot in the classroom and choose a different coin - perhaps a harder one - to cover it with. The children can compare how much their foot is worth with their hand. They can work out the difference between each other's hands, and they can add up how much a whole group of hands is worth! This will involve a great deal of addition, some subtraction and maybe some multiplication. Coins will be recognized, added, and exchanged.

**Fig. 5.5**

The results of this survey will supply a pool of information which can be used in the classroom. The children will discuss their data, they will need to analyse it and subsequently decide how best to display it. Because the children collected the information themselves, because it is **their** data, they will mind about how it is presented. Misleading or confusing methods of representation will be rejected and better ones discovered. The volume and capacity aspect of their work at home can lead to some comparison and or measurement in class. This will also need to be recorded in some way.

 **Blow-Out**

How many candles would you have blown out by now, if you have always had the correct number of candles on your birthday cake each year?

Can you work out how many candles someone else in your family would have blown out?

**Fig. 5.6**

In this activity the children are practising some of the skills which have formed a part of their maths in class. In the context of an investigation they will count, add and estimate. They will also be thinking and talking about the ideas of age and time passing - both difficult ideas for a small child to handle.

**Think about it**

*The advantages of involving parents in the curriculum through the use of shared activities are numerous:*

**i)** *The children have to explain and discuss some of the maths that they are studying at school. The talk involved here is very helpful in enhancing learning and developing their understanding.*

**ii)** *The children are constantly transferring mathematical skills from one context to another.*

**iii)** *The attitudes of both parents and the children to maths are likely to improve.*

**iv)** *The teacher can introduce activities and tasks which it would be impossible or impractical to do in the class with thirty children.*

## Parental involvement and the delivery of the National Curriculum

Building a partnership with parents through such schemes as PACT and IMPACT can only assist teachers in their delivery of the National Curriculum. The relationship between parents and teachers is greatly improved by the parents' involvement in their children's learning. Parents are much more likely to understand the things that their children are finding difficult and the areas in which they are making good progress. Teachers know that they can ask for and rely upon support and assistance from the home.

The teacher is better able to cover the enormous curriculum set out in all the documents of the Working Groups. Some Attainment Targets in particular cry out for the involvement of the home:

'Children should collect and find similarities and differences in a variety of everyday materials, natural and manufactured, including cooking ingredients...' (5.8)
'Children should explore ways in which good health can be promoted...they should investigate some aspects of feeding, support, movement and behaviour in relation to themselves and other animals...' (5.9)

Through this type of parental involvement, children will find themselves discussing their work, talking about what they learn and explaining things to other people. All these skills not only enhance learning and cognitive development, but they also are required as skills in their own right within the National Curriculum.

# ▢ Summary

In this chapter we have considered the following aspects of National Curriculum delivery:

1   The National Curriculum has organizational implications. How teachers organize their classrooms and their choice of teaching approach will be influenced by:
    Programmes of Study;
    the demands of assessment;
    the recommendations of NCC.
2   Teachers must consider three types of pedagogy. These can be considered under three headings; class teaching, individual teaching and group work. The latter have many advantages for good National Curriculum delivery.
3   It is important to involve parents at all stages in the delivery of the National Curriculum. Some of the easiest means of doing this are described in schemes such as PACT or IMPACT.

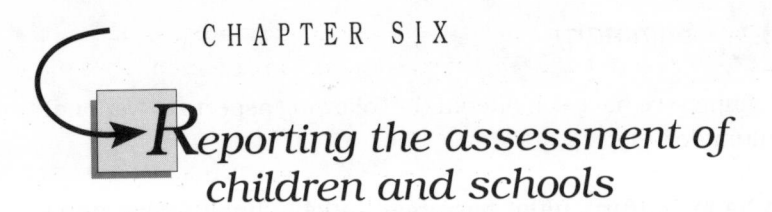

CHAPTER SIX

# Reporting the assessment of children and schools

THIS chapter deals with reporting processes in the National Curriculum and is split into three sections.

*Section 1* introduces and deals with the scope of reporting back.
*Section 2* provides an outline of the reporting back procedures within the context of the structure of the National Curriculum as a whole.
*Section 3* discusses areas of concern that have been raised in many parts of the country about the implications and consequences of reporting the results of assessment.

We discuss National Curriculum reporting dispassionately. Official documents emphasize the 'needs' of those 'entitled' to the information we review below. We do not seek to infringe those, in many ways, hard won entitlements. On the other hand, teachers are worried.

They are not worried that what they hitherto have managed 'to conceal' will now be revealed, but that reporting may misrepresent what they do. Before we can see where we are in the midst of all these concerns we must first establish the basic processes involved in reporting.

## Section 1: The scope of reporting

A fundamental change will take place in the practice of reporting the results of assessments to parents, governors and outside agencies. The scope of reporting back will be much more extensive than ever before. In addition, there will be much more information about the school and its curriculum to which parents will have access, as well as information that they will be receiving as a matter of course.

Reporting is a key part of the National Curriculum process. It is not supplementary. It will have a formative part to play in shaping the curriculum of the school and its policies.

Reporting will place the results of a school's assessments in a context such that parents, governors and outside agencies may make **comparisons** between classrooms, schools and LEAS.

Detailed information about the overall attainment of a classroom, of a school, and of an LEA will be available to parents, prospective parents, and the DES. Grouped information (data that has been' aggregated') about schools will have a wide public circulation.

## National Assessment will affect all school life

The ERA increases the accountability of the teaching profession to both its paymasters (the tax-payer via the treasury via the DES), and what are now being increasingly defined as its 'consumers', i.e. parents. Reporting back to these groups is going to be an integral part of the assessment process.

National Assessment will affect and in some cases be the final arbiter in decisions to be made about:

❑ individual children;
❑ classroom organization;
❑ syllabus construction;
❑ allocation of resources;
❑ curricula emphasis;
❑ admissions policy;
❑ teacher careers.

**It will be the same assessment information derived from children that will be used to contribute to the evaluations of schools and LEAs.**

While this may sound grim we should be careful not to tar the notion of assessment in education with the same brush we use to tar the traditional **mis-use** of assessment.

## Section 2: An outline of National Curriculum reporting

There are three main types of information which will be made available to parents, the DES and the public under the provisions of ERA:

i) From school to individual parents: curricular details and assessment details about individual children;

ii) From school to particular outside agencies:staffing, financial, curricular and assessment details, grouped for classes and schools;

iii) The school prospectus will contain comparative assessment data.

Every year schools will be processing assessment information and reporting the outcome on all children who have reached the **Key Reporting Ages** in their school careers (at 7, 11, 14 and 16). The information will be used in the variety of contexts listed above. This assessment information will also be used as an evaluation index of the school.

The diagram opposite illustrates the process by which the assessment information is packaged in various ways to be presented to the listed recipients. Other information that schools are liable to provide is described below in the sections dealing with schools and parents. The National Curriculum makes provision for what should happen at each stage of the depicted reporting process.

## Stage 1: Processing assessment information

Processing the assessment data will be carried out according to the advice given with the assessment materials themselves. Schools will have carried out two types of **moderation**:

i) the moderation by SATs of continuous assessment data, and

ii) the moderation of teacher estimates after teachers have discussed each other's assessment results with examples of work. This discussion will first of all take place between the teachers in each school and will then be widened to include inter-school discussion.

The Reporting Process

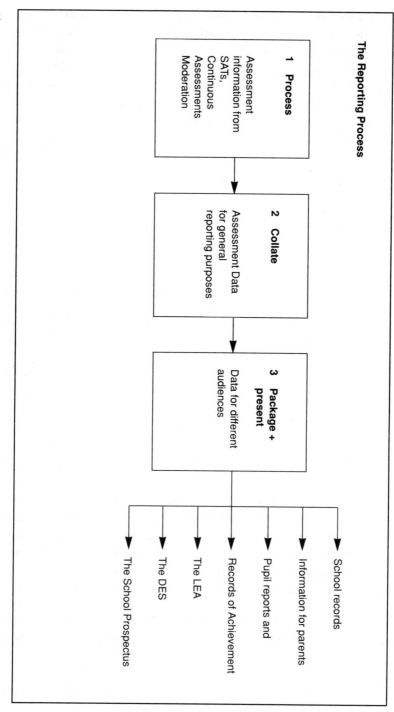

**1 Process**

Assessment information from SATs, Continuous Assessments Moderation

**2 Collate**

Assessment Data for general reporting purposes

**3 Package + present**

Data for different audiences

School records

Information for parents

Pupil reports and

Records of Achievement

The LEA

The DES

The School Prospectus

Fig 6.1

Teachers will have the following:

**i)** an assessment of each child on each profile component. They will have collected evidence of children's performances on a large number of Statements of Attainment within the relevant Attainment Targets.
This assessment information will be aggregated. Firstly teachers will summarize the information from Statements of Attainment to Attainment Targets. Secondly, they will summarize from Attainment Targets to Profile Components. Thirdly, the information may be aggregated into levels for each subject.

**ii)** an assessment of the class (or group of 'reportable children') which will take the form of a set of 'distributions'.

An example of a distribution is as follows:

**Key Report Stage 1**                    **CLASS 3**

English Profile Component 2:

| **LEVEL** | 1 | 2 | 3 |
|-----------|------|------|------|
|           | 8%   | 80%  | 12%  |

These are **aggregated** results for a class.
Parents will get the results for their own children plus the grouped data for the class. This is to enable parents to compare the outcomes of assessments of their child with the results for the class as a whole.

## Stage 2: Collating assessment data for general reporting

We have to end up with assessment data, about individual children in the first instance, which has been collated, organized, processed and displayed in very similar ways.

In Chapter Three we saw that there were versatile methods of record-keeping which help foster teaching practices commensurate with the National Curriculum. However, ERA seeks to make **national**

**comparisons**. Eventually there will be a standardized format for the collection and collation of assessment data.

The consultation document on Section 22 of ERA states that there is a '...need for central agreement on the form in which statistical data is collected and presented, to allow for national and local aggregations and analysis, and the case for nationally produced pro-formas to underpin this.'

It will be the duty of the school to collate all information necessary for the reporting requirements of Section 22 of ERA. Until nationally standardized 'pro-formas' are in place, schools will make their own arrangements in their National Curriculum Development Plans.

The purpose of these 'collation' forms is to facilitate the movement of information between the various agencies cited in this chapter. The 'pro-formas' will shunt information between governing bodies, LEAs and the DES.

Comparability is a prime objective of ERA and National Assessment has to be standardized. It is projected that nationally produced forms will be made available for the purposes of **recording** as well as **collating** assessment data. This has the following implications:

1   Eventually there will be a temptation for teachers to use more 'standard tasks' which make agreements as to the level of children's performances on the various Statements of Attainment easier to obtain. Commercially-produced materials rather than teacher-created or drafted activities will make consensus more readily achieved.

2   At present schools may choose their own, National Curriculum-compatible form of keeping records. However, the desire to minimize the work involved in transferring assessment information from one form or record to another, will inevitably lead to a much more standardized approach to the keeping of classroom records.

3   Some of the assessment recording mechanisms will be given as standard formats by SEAC. These will have an effect upon the range and scope of the curriculum content covered in depth and also upon the teaching methods used.

## Stage 3:  The packaging and presentation of assessment data

Assessment data is packaged so that those in receipt of the information are able to analyse the data for the purposes of decision-making as well as for routine monitoring.

The school will find greater design implications in presenting assessment data to its **consumers** than it will to its managers. It is for parents and prospective parents that the reforms of Section 22 were included in ERA.

Section 22 compels radical changes to all ways in which schools report and present themselves. Stage 3 involves:

**i)**  changes to traditional school reports and
**ii)**  the introduction of reporting previously unavailable information.

These changes concern:

**A**  school records;
**B**  information for parents;
**C**  pupil reports and records of achievement;
**D**  information at the LEA;
**E**  information at the DES;
**F**  the school prospectus (prospective parents).

### A  School records

As we have stated throughout this book the results of assessment for each pupil will need to be diligently kept. Such records will contain:

❏  details of the exact syllabus followed by the pupil;
❏  details of all Attainment Targets attempted, including quite specific information as to which Statements of Attainment were focussed upon;
❏  the level on which the pupil is on all prescribed Attainment Targets, again including the details of the child's performance on specified Statements of Attainment;

❏ details of any activities which do not fall under the prescriptions of the National Curriculum, but which have nevertheless formed part of the pupil's school experience.

These records are for use by the school in planning the next syllabus for the pupil. They are confidential. No-one has a right to see them except those professionally concerned with the pupil's education and the pupil's parents. Those 'professionally concerned' are the LEA and the governing body of the school. But, in the act, these two bodies have a right to the information about individual children to the extent that the information is relevant to the 'performance by that body of authority of any of their functions'. (Section 22, Para. 5)

In practice, the individual pupil records will need to be available to:

1   each pupil's parents;
2   the next teacher to teach the child;
3   the headteacher who needs to know individual results in order to monitor pupils' progress and make curriculum and management decisions.

## B Information for parents

Many of these changes in education are coming about, it is said, with parents in mind. Parents will be receiving information about their children's school, curriculum, management and assessment **as a matter of course**. They are also in a position to see, on demand, the more detailed information about their children's individual syllabus. Schools will be required to provide:

❏ a copy of each child's 'Programme of Study' for the year ahead;
❏ details of Attainment Targets planned for the year;
❏ whether SATs are to be set;
❏ details of any other tests;
❏ details of any departures from, or additions to, the National Curriculum.

Parents will be in a position to judge their children's performances against national standards, as well as, of course, the 'performance' of the school in terms of the outcomes of National Assessments.

Parents should also be able to see how their child is doing in respect of his/her own previous performances.

### C Individual children's reports

## Pupil reports and records of achievement

It is envisaged that, **at the least**, parents will have for their own child at each key stage, a statement of assessment results for each foundation subject, **along with some comparative data**.' (6.1 - our emphasis).

The form of presentation of individual reports is being designed. The clear directive of ERA is that parents should be able to see not only where their children are on the Attainment Target ladders, but also where their children are in relation to where the majority of their peers are on those ladders.

A parent will, therefore, be able to make comparisons between their child and his/her schoolmates (treated collectively), in terms of their progress through the National Curriculum. Such comparisons will be possible within the same school, within the LEA and conceivably across the whole country.

Assessment data will form part of a report containing the more usual 'pastoral' information.

## Records of achievement

Development work has been carried out over the past five years to produce standardized documents for school-leavers which are a more all-round account of their education and development than examination results. The purposes of records of achievement were outlined in a 1984 policy statement:

1   Recognition of achievement - both academic as well as other achievements during school career;

**2** Motivation and personal development;

**3** Curriculum and organization - as much an evaluation of the school as the pupil;

**4** A document of record.

It is envisaged that all pupils' National Assessments will be included in the summative record (6.1). Most of the record 'developers' planned to record achievement in curriculum subjects as well as the 'acquisition of general learning skills' before ERA was written. So there are parallels in approach.

The advice given to teachers by SEAC does specifically mention records of achievement; 'It has been recommended that records of achievement are used as a vehicle for recording progress and achievement within the National Curriculum system throughout the years of compulsory schooling.' (6.1)

Records of achievement have been found to be more valuable when pupils and parents play an active role in their compilation. It was further recommended that they should focus upon positive achievement. It is to be hoped that the methods of reporting National Assessment outcomes will be such as to continue the development of records of achievement.

## D  Information at the Local Education Authority

Reporting to the LEA will take the form of aggregated results for classroom groups of pupils for the evaluation of individual teachers. Aggregations of class distributions can make one whole school set of distributions for each Profile Component.

ERA has brought about a number of changes which mean that LEAs now require this information.

### i) Evaluating the LEA

The LEA is being 'evaluated' against other LEAs in the country in terms of its performance in 'levering up' its pupil population to higher Levels of Attainment. Assessment reporting here is going to be thought of as a standard index of performance for an LEA prior to any mitigating circumstances such as the socio-economic condition of its population.

## ii) Changes to the role of the LEA

Responsibility for curriculum policy is shifting from LEAs to the Governing bodies of schools. 'Grant-aided' and 'special agreement' schools need have 'only a regard' to LEA curriculum policies when deciding their own. Primarily, 'the LEA is responsible for **monitoring** and **facilitating** the provision of the school curriculum, including the National Curriculum in the schools which it maintains'. (6.1 - our emphasis).

## iii) Local Management of Schools (LMS)

The new arrangements connect assessment with the financial management of schools in new ways through the medium of reporting back.

A system has been set up known as the Local Management of Schools (or LMS). Schools with over 200 pupils are normally required to manage their own finances. Schools with less than this number of pupils may continue to have their finances co-ordinated by the LEA. Schools who fall under LMS will report directly to the Secretary of State information regarding finances, while the remaining LEA schools report to their LEAs who then pass on aggregated information to the DES.

The network for reporting financial information will be used to report information about assessment as well as other information which we will discuss below.

The idea that distributions of the aggregated outcomes of assessment will be used to evaluate LEAs, schools and even specific teachers, is a cause for concern amongst many in education. Fears have been expressed that 'the information on assessment outcomes will be reduced to league tables in the local press.' SEAC expresses the pious if ill-founded hope that 'just as schools and teachers need to learn how to create and interpret alternative forms of criterion-referenced reports, so does the wider community'. There are many who feel that positive and practical steps must be taken by teachers and other educationalists if we are to avoid the worst effects of such a scenario. Such steps might include:

- building a partnership with parents based on shared approaches to learning through schemes such as PACT or paired reading;
- including as much useful information as possible in any school reports or brochures;
- creating positive links between the school and the local community through sharing resources;
- adopting a policy of partnership with other local schools rather than competition.

## E Information at the Department of Education and Science

The National Curriculum is defined as an 'entitlement'. Assessment will play a key role in determining whether or not teachers, schools, governing bodies and LEAs have fulfilled their obligations with respect to that entitlement. We now have a system which could decide the 'viability' of a school in terms of resources, management and curriculum delivery.

In terms of the decision-making processes regulated by the act, the following information about schools' curriculum provision will need to be passed from the governing bodies to the LEA and the Secretary of State.

- Subject offered and time spent on them for all age groups;
- How the curriculum is organized:    cross-curricular, integrated, modular etc;
- Length of school day showing time spent 'actually teaching' as opposed to other activities;
- Numbers of pupils for whom the National Curriculum has been modified or disapplied;
- Staff used to deliver the curriculum, showing use of their time, subject by subject, in relation to their qualifications and relevant INSET experience.

The forms necessary to enable schools to provide this information are being supplied by the DES. There is currently much dispute over the construction of these forms and the difficulties they present. Some primary headteachers are firmly convinced that it remains impossible to provide some of the information required with any reasonable degree of accuracy. For example, it may not be possible to break down the teaching in a reception class into the categories specified. It remains to be seen if the requirement that this information be provided has an effect upon the teaching methods employed or simply upon the modes of information provision.

## F  The school prospectus

A school's means of presenting itself to its intended consumers and other interested parties will be in a prospectus containing increasingly standardized information. There will be much more in the prospectus that will be of a comparative nature. It is envisaged that, in the context of open enrolment, schools will construct their prospectuses in order to attract potential customers.

A school will have to make available in both the prospectus and its governors' reports, the aggregated results of assessment at the key stages. For the First Key Stage, 7 years, this will not be a requirement but 'desirable'. For other key stages publication of results in LEA maintained schools is a legal requirement.

The precise 'look' of this information is the subject of consultation at the time of writing, but it is proposed that it will:

'...be in a standard format, but...should not include any pupils to whom the National Curriculum was not fully applied in the subject in question'.
Whatever format is ultimately used to report this data, we can expect breakdowns 'subject by subject' to be included. The LEA has to make available aggregations of results concerning all its schools.

## Section 3:   Areas of concern

In all parts of England and Wales concern has been expressed about the new system of assessment and the manner in which it will be reported. It is accepted that assessment can be both useful and positive if it is 'formative'. The problems arise as schools start to consider the effects of reporting when assessment information will be used **comparatively**.

There are two main areas of concern:

**i)** How to cope with the demands of reporting and presenting information;

**ii)** What will be the effect on schools, their clients and communities?

## I Reporting:  content and presentation

We can foresee a number of problems with the reporting back aspects of the National Curriculum. However, this means that we can to some extent also deal with these, or at least make some provision for these, in advance. Forseeable problems include:

**a)** teacher evaluation on too narrow a basis;
**b)** the direct comparison of schools;
**c)** the devaluing of the social and economic background of a school in the light of assessment outcomes;
**d)** records of Achievement and GCSEs.

### Problem A - teacher evaluation

The National Curriculum is all about children progressing though the 10 levels as far as they can get. Reporting makes it possible to say **where** children are at **any** time.

At Key Reporting Ages the aggregated distribution for a class will be an appraisal of a teacher. Teachers' distributions say **where** their class is on the Attainment Levels. This outcome is directly comparable to teachers of similar classes. The information **does not** contain information about how the children were distributed on the levels **when the children first entered their custody.**

### Causes

National Assessment has been set up to deal with **progression** over large periods called key stages. In such a large period of two or three years, criteria of attainment can be specified in advance.

Teachers and parents tend to put queries about assessment in smaller time-frames. It is more difficult in smaller time-frames to set out detailed criteria of attainment in advance. Also, teachers and parents tend to see a child's Level of Attainment in terms of 'ability'.

The provisions for **reporting** National Assessment do not include the time-frame within which primary teachers make assessment judgements, neither do they include a facility for showing differential **rates** of progress **within** a key stage. Reporting will make direct comparisons of teachers at fixed moments of time.

Teachers are responsible for the **overall** education of the children in their care. They may spend a great deal of time and effort improving social and emotional behaviour, and enhancing children's development in ways not directly assessed by the National Curriculum. All these aspects of education, felt to be of crucial importance by parents and teachers alike, are ignored by National Curriculum assessment except in so far as children's improved behaviour or emotional state assists their progress up the attainment ladders. This aspect of a teacher's work is ignored if the sole basis for teacher evaluation is the distribution of assessment outcomes.

## What we need to work towards

Reported assessment data **could** include rate of progress if it were to be collected and computed in the first place. So, data on **rate** of progression would need to be part of the computations that occur during the assessment process itself (see Chapter Four). SEAC would need to advise us on how this would be done after having carried out research and development work through one of its commissioned agencies. Some of these agencies are currently working on this and the advice given by SEAC does include some aspects of progression monitoring.

Information about distributions could **always** be given in the context of further information about teachers and their classes. For example, it could include such details as the numbers of children with social or behavioural difficulties, the number with English as a second language, the turn-over of children in the class, and so on. Qualitative methods of appraisal can be used to monitor children's progress in other areas than National Curriculum attainment.

Parents are always concerned about the emotional and social well-being of their children, and also about such things as their attitudes to learning and so on. If teachers have enabled children to progress in these areas, this should be made an explicit part of the evaluation of their work.

## Problem B - Direct comparison of schools

A related problem to teacher appraisal is raised in the business of **comparing** schools and LEAs. Aggregated data across all Key Reporting Age-pupils has to be made available by the school. It is based on the same assessment data as in Problem A.

It would be fairer if we had a sense of how far pupils have come, given their starting points. A school that appears to be 'doing well' in that it has an above average number of pupils at 7 in Level 3 may **not** actually be 'performing as well as' a school which has a below average number of pupils at Level 3. The second school **may** have been starting out with a population of pupils aged 5 whose skills on entry did not facilitate their rapid acceleration through the first three levels.

### Example

Imagine a school in an inner city deprived area. Perhaps many of the children are bi-lingual. Contrast this with a small village school in an affluent part of the South-East. We can imagine the tables of distribution of results to be as follows:

**School 1**

| Level | 1 | 2 | 3 |
|---|---|---|---|
| | 20% | 75% | 5% |

**School 2**

| Level | 1 | 2 | 3 |
|---|---|---|---|
| | 10% | 40% | 50% |

In this situation, it will appear that School 1 comes pretty poorly out of the comparison. However, a sensible 'consumer' will want to know what the base line for this comparison consists of. Firstly, how many children are we talking about in each case? Secondly, at what level were the children when they came to school?

Suppose that the first school has 90 children at reporting age 7, and the second school has 10 children at this stage. Suppose also that of those 10 children, 5 were assessed as being at Level 2 upon entry to the school, and one child was at Level 3. The comparison now starts to look very different. If we add that 90% of the children in the first school enter the school without having yet acquired, in English at least, the skills necessary to achieve Level 1, then the teachers in the first school can be said to be achieving a rate of progress of over 70% of children moving at least two levels in two years - i.e. considerably above the national average. Whilst in the second school, several children do not appear to have progressed at all.

## Solution

The only solutions would be to:

i)  adopt a means of recording rate of progress in continuous assessment as in Problem A, which recorded and reported the skill baselines of pupils;
ii)  effect standardized adjustments to comparative data based on the social contexts of the schools in question;
iii)  attempt to report all distributions as one aspect only of a more complete report on a school. This will encourage parents, and others, to see these distributions as one piece of information amongst many upon which a school's performance must be judged, rather than the sole criteria for evaluation.

## Problem C - The social and economic background of a school is devalued in the light of assessment

Contextual information about the school will not be included in the calculation of assessment data. Therefore comparisons of distributions between schools will read as if the schools were starting from the same neutral ground.

## Background

The government will be taking advice on such things as '...ground-rules for aggregation, use of socio-economic contextual data, etc...' (6.1). However, we can take it as read that methods used for scoring and calculating assessment data **will not** include 'contextual' information - which includes, for the forseeable future, information about a child's rate of progress.

IN THE MEANTIME

socio-economic information about the school may be included in its prospectus and such information will be communicated as a rider to assessment results.

## Problem D - Records of achievement and GCSEs

A great deal of work has gone into the design of records of achievement and GCSEs. There are fears that both will disappear in the wake of National Assessment.

## Background

### i) Records of achievement

During development of records of achievement it was noted how useful 'interim' reports were in forming the final record. Reports such as these emerge traditionally in the pattern of the school year and usually in relation to particular curricula events.
However, in the future it will be National Assessment which will 'give the pattern' for how and when summary records are arrived at and processed despite the stated need for information about a pupil other than the assessment sort.

It can be argued that the entire character of records of achievement will form differently in the environment of the National Curriculum. The Records of Achievement Steering Committee (RANSC) recorded that pupils and parents place considerable importance on the summary document and that, in the pilot studies, it may have been the 'principle motivator' of pupils.

With the advent of regular standardized assessment, the patterns of motivation among pupils and their parents can change considerably. The effect would be to increase the gap between the 'assessment information' and 'pastoral information'. The two forms of information sit more closely together at the moment in the eyes of the parents, pupils and employers because of the marked absence of long term, national and **comparative** forms of assessment.

Further, records of achievement have stressed the involvement of the pupils themselves and their parents in the final summative document as well as at all interim stages. The importance of focussing upon positive achievement has also been stressed. Neither of these two aspects of the work of RANSC appears to have any place in the structure of National Assessment reporting. Lip-service is paid to the views of parents and to discussion with pupils, but whether a school or teacher talks at all to either, the National Assessment will proceed regardless and its outcomes will be **reported** to parents and children.

Given the importance of the work of RANSC and the information they have presented concerning the effects of reporting assessment upon the motivation of pupils, it is imperative that schools, teachers and parents continue to work developing Records of Achievement as envisaged by RANSC within the context of National Assessment.

## ii) GCSEs

It has been suggested that Level 10 of the National Curriculum should be construed as the peak of attainment in any target to be expected of a 16 year-old. Therefore the top grade of a GCSE should be equivalent to a Level 10 attainment.

The assessment system has been designed so that 'loosely bundled' Attainment Targets at the beginning of a school career will tighten up as a child approaches 14 to form Attainment Target bundles more closely resembling the traditional 'subjects' of the curriculum.

The Act itself does not provide for the phasing out of the GCSE and many people are not sure why the pundits predict its demise. This prediction has to do with:

**i)** the incompatibility of **how** and **what** is assessed in the current GCSE with **how** and **what** will be assessable in the National Curriculum;

**ii)** the way in which the curricula content material was offered to the Secretaries of State by the subject working parties.

### Projection

The extent to which GCSEs and records of achievement are either incompatible with or do not facilitate National Assessment has yet to be seen.

National Assessment will have a heavy cost in labour and time in itself. Additional recording burdens will not be welcomed.

It is expected that the Fourth Key Reporting Stage (16 years) will be certificated.

## ⬜ II The effects of reporting

There are fears that wide reporting of assessments without background information will reflect badly on many schools. In response to this, schools might look at assessment only from a 'cosmetic' point of view.

The fears stem from perceiving that National Assessment seems to focus too narrowly on skills and performance. Furthermore, it is feared that such a narrow focus will have dire consequences for the quality of commercial schemes used in schools.
Part II looks at:

**a)** the desired effects of reporting;
**b)** the emphasis on skills, and
**c)** commercial schemes and consumer behaviour.

## a) The positive side to reporting

Under the provisions of ERA it should:

**i)** be possible to reach a position where both parents and teachers are using the same language to discuss such things as the curriculum, progression, weaknesses, etc...
This language would be universal in England and Wales.

**ii)** be easier for parents to question the education process itself and from a position of some expertize in educational organisation. Parents should be able to make judgements about the type of approach a school or teacher takes to their child.

**iii)** enable parents to have a clearer view of **where** their child is, comparatively speaking. At present, a parent tends to **hear** how well their child is doing **in relation to others**, when what they are **being told** is how well he is doing **'for him'**. This has led to much talk at cross-purposes in home-school dialogue, and to problems that stay hidden until crucial assessments occur.

**iv)** be simpler for parents and schools when seeking external advice; to agree and prepare their case, to be mutually clear about objectives and to evaluate the advice they have been given.

**v)** be simpler from the school's point of view to explain their approach and consult with parents about curricular choices at some level of detail.

## Problems

The positive aspects of reporting all relate to the home-school dialogue. Given the format of National Assessment reporting the following problems arise:

**i)** The structure of reporting with its emphasis on local and national comparability, may make it more difficult for the teacher to focus a parent's anxiety about their children's achievements on their particular rate of progression.

**ii)** For reporting purposes, parents, and others receive 'aggregated' scores grouped for convenience into 'Profile Components'. A teacher's difficulty in helping a child towards certain curricula objectives is better expressed at the level of Attainment Targets and Statements of Attainment rather than Profile Components.

Attainment Targets are closer to a school's curriculum and represent the particular choices and curricula emphasis embarked upon.

## b) An emphasis on skills

ERA increases the visibility of **skills** for teachers and parents. Certain specified skills will become the major **signposts** of education itself.

In the past the teaching profession has failed to give a high status to what it sees as 'skills'. These are too often viewed by teachers as things acquired through 'rote learning'. But rote learning merely defines **one method of acquiring** a skill. This association of skills with rote learning is, we think, a popular misconception among teachers.

Nevertheless, by making skills the only available **description** of education, we invite serious consequences for how we conduct the educative process.

ERA sees progression as the laying down of large scale teaching and learning compaigns where certain key 'skill groupings' define the boundaries between levels.

It is more than possible that these 'boundary skill-groupings' become the **objectives** of the teaching plans. This is a subtle shift of emphasis which would serve to narrow the curriculum if not checked. The curriculum Working Parties hope that their documents will be seen as **outlines** of the content to be covered. The skills they use to illustrate what a child should be able to do at any point or on any level should be seen as signposts.

## Causes of concern

i)   The focus on skills is, we must remember, a source of feedback to the teachers of how others read their performance.
ii)  The attainment of skills is what parents will be looking for evidence of - especially in relation to the schemes of work which schools have to provide for their parents.
iii) TGAT recommended that assessment of these skills should be a **hidden** part of a child's school life. However well the tests are

designed and administered, parents will be rightly **forewarned** of them.

## c) 'Consumer behaviour' and reporting - a discussion

Already material calibrated to the National Curriculum Levels of Attainment is being produced for use in homes. It could make a school's distributions of assessment results more 'attractive', or it could increase variability among children. Will these new materials for use in the home be used to 'push' children who would have been in the high levels of attainment anyway into even higher levels?

The Act sets up a complaints procedure that parents may use if they feel their children are not getting their entitlement. We may speculate on the words and terms of such complaints - will they boil down to a dispute of the possession or non-possession of certain skills? Will skills themselves be the boundaries at which parental disputes are levied at schools?

Schools in their turn could, in their own 'best interests', be careful to screen for skills in prospective pupils. Such a climate could induce school-parent competition and rivalry rather than a spirit of collaboration.

The structure of the National Curriculum in the long term, being 'regulated' by an educational 'economy of skills', could collapse from its own competitive momentum. We are all familiar with the phenomenon of new knowledge and skills eventually filtering 'down' into the 14+ syllabuses for 16+ public examinations and so on. We are also familiar with children who are pushed to achieve educational attainments 'ahead of their ages'. A combination of these two tendencies in somewhat milder forms could operate in the context of the National Curriculum.

New skills will ultimately come to define what Levels 8, 9 and 10 actually are. The new goal-posts will have a more profound effect on the entire 5-16 curriculum than they could have had in the past with the latter's more diversified base. SEAC's own document (Sourcebook on Teacher Assessment) points out that development through the levels of the National Curriculum cannot be uniform - we do not grow at the same rate through each of the levels. Whatever the reasons are for this, it is clear that the greatest care and attention must be given to how we communicate and contextualize information about a child's acquisition of skills.

Much of this acquisition is unseen and not communicable. We should be wary of over-simplified diagrams like the one in the TGAT report plotting age against levels of the National Curriculum. It was meant to be only an illustration but mistaken by many to represent actual findings, or facts.

Inattention to such things, far from 'levering up' the population's competence would lever up the population's 'image' of competence.

Let it be understood that there is nothing necessary about the current system of levels in terms of what defines their boundaries. At this stage in the deployment of the National Curriculum, the Attainment Targets levels as we have received them are a reasonable reflection of what we might expect of pupils. If a spiral of inflation in the 'economy of skills' set in, then we could have little confidence in systems of assessment that would, perforce, have to 'run behind' a nation's obsession with visible competence.

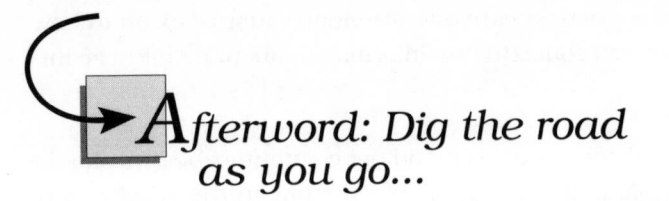

# Afterword: Dig the road as you go...

NOW is the moment to pause, to take our leave of one another and speculate about the road ahead. While we can never be sure exactly what will happen next in education, we can all make intelligent statements about the future. In this book we have iterated and reiterated our 'rule of thumb'. Once you grasp the principle that the National Curriculum is founded on a system of assessment into which everything else has to fit you cannot go far wrong.

All the details of assessment will indeed change over the years so that what we get in 1992 may not clearly correspond with what we shall see in 2002. **But** while ERA stands in its current form the very framework of the curriculum is **defined** by the system by which it is assessed.

## Assessment is not necessarily bad news

We should not be afraid of assessment - it is meant to be there as a guide and source of feedback to what we are doing in the classroom. For years, many thinking of the children, parents and teachers, and with their best interests at heart, have asked for an intelligent assessment process to operate side-by-side with the curriculum.

The authors of this book believe that using assessment as the framework of a curriculum could be a positive **aid** to teachers if it helped to plan, organize a class of children, keep useful records and assess against shared criteria.

## ◻ Assessing a skills-based curriculum

Assessment can be a good thing. A skills-based curriculum could be a good thing. It becomes a bad thing when a curriculum is 'skills-only'. In this event, we no longer have a curriculum concerned with what we traditionally mean by education. What we have then is a curriculum of 'utilities' for which children become the repositories.

If the National Curriculum suffers from any major flaws in respect of what education is all about then it consists in this:   that it is an ingeniously designed system of processes and mechanisms all of which we can train ourselves to see clearly and to implement, but whose consequences, effects, aims and intentions remain shrouded in fog. The National Curriculum is educationally blind. Its blindness consists in teachers not being able to articulate for themselves what they are doing in educationally relevant terms. The National Curriculum has a language for talking about the nuts and bolts, but we do not know who is driving the car or where it is going.

No further bulletins from NCC or SEAC will clarify **that** situation. And that's where you come in. You have been given the tools, now you must dig the road. Within the context of the National Curriculum we must begin again to re-think what education is for ourselves. We must not say, 'It's too late to discuss such things now' - it is never the time to stop talking, re-thinking, imagining and talking again.

In the course of this book, we have tried to provide some of the tools with which you can dig the road. In Chapters Three, Four and Five, we suggested how the planning, classroom organization and record-keeping could fit around the assessment process. The mechanisms outlined, whilst complying with the demands of ERA, still allow for flexibility of teaching style, a wide choice of materials and individual approaches. We showed how the National Curriculum, although to a large extent it does dictate **what** we have to teach, still leaves the decision as to **how** to teach firmly in the hands of classroom teachers.

Prior to the publication of this book, we have been involved in the delivery of a great deal of National Curriculum INSET. From Humberside to Devon, from West Glamorgan to East London, we have been describing the framework of the National Curriculum and discussing its implications with teachers. We have also participated in INSET given by a number of different speakers and noted the questions asked by teachers. We have listened to the increasing concern expressed about the ERA, about the National Curriculum, about what teachers are being asked to deliver, the terms of its delivery, and how it is to be reported.

In a recent session, a teacher summed up for us the experiences of all this in-service training. About ten minutes from the end, just as the session was winding down, she said, 'Oh, I do **hate** these INSETs. Every single one that I've been to finishes in the same way. We all get into a discussion about the National Curriculum, and I go home feeling totally depressed. The fun has gone right out of teaching. It all seems completely hopeless.' We were shocked by this outburst. We felt that if this was true about National Curriculum INSET, then no matter what information was successfully imparted, it did much more harm than good in terms of the damage to teachers' commitment and enthusiasm. Most teachers are in the profession because they have a commitment to a certain view of education. They believe in its importance and find a personal joy and satisfaction in children's learning.

The ERA appears to ride roughshod through these beliefs. It seems to treat children as bundles of assessable criteria, and education as the inculcation of specified skills. But we feel that all is not hopeless and that we should not leave feeling depressed.

We have tried to emphasize that teachers still have an immense amount of control, both on a day-to-day basis in terms of what goes on in the classroom, but also on a year-to-year basis in terms of planning the curriculum.

Neither children nor parents change instantly and dramatically as a result of the passing of a law. Classrooms will still retain their liveliness and we can still enable children to enjoy learning and to make discoveries for themselves. Parents will still be grateful for teachers' efforts, and some will continue to express their gratitude.

We have a certain well-founded faith in the ability of people to alter, adapt and mould structures designed by outsiders so that they become comfortable to live in and something quite other than their designers intended.

Whatever the 'designers'' intentions were, we are now enmeshed in a welter of contested statements about education and the nature of the National Curriculum. Parents, teachers and governors have been buried beneath a large heap of bureaucratic, financial and curricular detail and LEAs have undergone major internal reorganization. In this book we have attempted to keep the basic mechanism of the new curriculum before us, while investigating its properties in the context of more familiar classroom strategies such as topic work.

As we have worked through the classroom strategies of curriculum organization and record-keeping, it has become manifestly clear that the immediate effect of ERA in schools is to focus attention increasingly on the **performances** of children and teachers. As they stand, the criteria of performance are narrowly defined and do not reflect the **work** that children and teachers actually do. However, the attempt to adequately reflect, within standardized and comparative assessment, the spectrum of activity to be found in the classroom is bound to be prohibitively expensive, time-consuming and counter-productive. Yet, to ditch an unwieldy assessment strategy (such as long SATs) in favour of 'quick tests' leaves the basic assessment process and its overall effects intact.

To believe that an assessment **technique** can provide an authentic comparison between the performances of children, teachers and schools, is to subscribe to a dangerous myth. Like the famous computer in *The Hitch-Hikers' Guide to the Galaxy* which, when asked the answer to the ultimate question of 'life, the universe and everything', replied, 'Forty-two', an assessment technique cannot reveal ultimate facts about human qualities or values. In the end, these intangible qualities and values are what characterize human interactions, including those that take place in schools.

Finally, the National Curriculum in practice is not yet written. As much as it depends on anyone, it depends on classroom teachers to dictate what its final shape will look like. First we must decide the direction, then we can continue to dig the road.

# MATHEMATICS NATIONAL CURRICULUM  ATTAINMENT TARGETS

| ATTAINMENT TARGET | LEVEL 1 |
|---|---|
| 1 USE NUMBER ALGEBRA AND MEASURES IN PRACTICAL TASKS, IN REAL-LIFE PROBLEMS, AND TO INVESTIGATE WITHIN MATHEMATICS ITSELF | Use materials provided for a task<br>Talk about own work and ask questions<br>Make predictions based on experience |
| 2 UNDERSTAND NUMBER AND NUMBER NOTATION | Count, read, write and order numbers to at least 10; know that the size of a set is given by the last number in the count<br>Understand the conservation of number |
| 3 UNDERSTAND NUMBER OPERATIONS (+, -, MULTIPLICATION AND DIVISION) AND MAKE USE OF APPROPRIATE METHODS OF CALCULATION | Add or subtract, using objects where the numbers involved are no greater than 10 |
| 4 ESTIMATE AND APPROXIMATE IN NUMBER | Give a sensible estimate of a small number of objects (up to 10) |
| 5 RECOGNIZE AND USE PATTERNS, RELATIONSHIPS AND SEQUENCES AND MAKE GENERALIZATIONS | Copy, continue and devise repeating patterns represented by objects/apparatus or one-digit numbers |
| 6 RECOGNIZE AND USE FUNCTIONS, FORMULAE, EQUATIONS AND INEQUALITIES | Nothing at this level |
| 7 USE GRAPHICAL REPRESENTATIONS OF ALGEBRAIC FUNCTIONS | Nothing at this level |
| 8 ESTIMATE AND MEASURE QUANTITIES AND APPRECIATE THE APPROXIMATE NATURE OF MEASUREMENT | Compare and order objects without measuring, and use appropriate language |
| 9 USE SHAPE AND SPACE AND HANDLE DATA IN PRACTICAL TASKS, IN REAL-LIFE PROBLEMS, AND TO INVESTIGATE WITHIN MATHEMATICS ITSELF | Use materials provided for a task<br>Talk about own work and answer questions<br>Make predictions based on experience |
| 10 RECOGNISE AND USE THE PROPERTIES OF TWO-DIMENSIONAL AND THREE-DIMENSIONAL SHAPES | Sort 3-D and 2-D shapes<br>Build with 3-D solid shapes and draw 2-D shapes and describe them |
| 11 RECOGNISE LOCATION AND USE TRANSFORMATIONS IN THE STUDY OF SPACE | State a position using prepositions such as; on, inside, above, under, behind, next to, etc.<br>Give and understand instructions for moving along a line. |
| 12 COLLECT,RECORD AND PROCESS DATA | Select criteria for sorting a set of objects and apply consistently |
| 13 REPRESENT AND INTERPRET DATA | Record with real objects or drawings and comment about the result<br>Create simple mapping diagrams showing relationships; read and interpret them |
| 14 UNDERSTAND, ESTIMATE AND CALCULATE PROBABILITIES | Recognize possible outcomes of simple random events |

*Fig. 4.4*

| LEVEL 2 | LEVEL 3 |
|---|---|
| Select the materials and the mathematics to use for a task<br>Describe current work, record findings and check results<br>Ask and respond to the question: 'What would happen if...?' | Select the materials and the mathematics to use for a task; check results and consider whether they are sensible<br>Explain work being done and record findings systematically<br>Make and test predictions |
| Read, write and order numbers to at least 100; use the knowledge that the tens-digit indicates the number of tens<br>Understand the meaning of 'a half' and 'a quarter' | Read, write and order numbers to at least 1000; use the knowledge that the position of a digit indicates its value<br>Use decimal notation as the conventional way of recording in money<br>Appreciate the meaning of negative whole numbers in familiar contexts |
| Know and use addition and subtraction facts up to 10<br>Compare two numbers to find the difference<br>Solve whole number problems involving addition and subtraction, including money | Know and use addition and subtraction number facts to 20 (including zero)<br>Solve problems involving multiplication or division of whole numbers or money, using a calculator where necessary<br>Know and use multiplication facts up to 5 x 5, and all those in 2, 5 and 10 multiplication tables |
| Make a sensible estimate of a number of objects up to 20 | Recognize that the first digit is the most important in indicating the size of a number, and approximate to the nearest 10 or 100<br>Understand 'remainders' given the context of calculation, and know whether to round up or down |
| Explore and use the patterns in addition and subtraction facts to 10<br>Distinguish between odd and even numbers | Explain number patterns and predict subsequent numbers where appropriate<br>Find number patterns and equivalent forms of 2-digit numbers and use these to perform mental calculations<br>Recognize whole numbers which are exactly divisible by 2, 5 and 10 |
| Understand the use of a symbol to stand for an unknown number | Deal with inputs and outputs from simple function machines |
| Nothing at this level | Nothing at this level |
| Use non-standard measures in length, area, volume, capacity, 'weight' and time to compare objects and recognize the need to use standard units<br>Know how to use coins in simple contexts<br>Know the most commonly used units in length, capacity, 'weight' and time and what they are used for | Use a wider range of metric units<br>Choose and use appropriate units and instruments in a variety of situations, interpreting numbers on a range of measuring instruments<br>Make and test predictions |
| Select the materials and the mathematics to use for a task<br>Describe current work, record findings and check results<br>Ask and respond to the question: 'What would happen if...?' | Select the materials and the mathematics to use for a task; check results and consider whether they are sensible<br>Explain work being done and record findings systematically<br>Make and test predictions |
| Recognize squares, rectangles, circles, triangles, hexagons, pentagons, cubes, rectangular boxes (cuboids), cylinders, spheres, and describe them<br>Recognize right-angled corners in; 2-D and 3-D shapes | Sort 2-D and 3-D shapes in different ways and give reasons for each method of sorting |
| Understand the notion of angle<br>Give and understand instructions for turning through right-angles<br>Recognize different types of movement: straight movement (translation); turning movement (rotation); flip movement (reflection) | Recognize the (reflective) symmetry in a variety of shapes in 2 and 3 dimensions<br>Understand eight points of the compass; use clockwise and anti-clockwise appropriately |
| Choose criteria to sort and classify objects; record results of observations or outcomes of events<br>Help to design a data collection sheet and use it to record a set of data leading to a frequency table | Extract specific pieces of information from tables and lists<br>Enter and access information in a simple database |
| Construct, read and interpret block graphs and frequency tables<br>Use diagrams to represent the result of classifying using two different criteria | Construct and interpret bar charts<br>Create and interpret graphs (pictograms) where the symbol represents a group of units |
| Recognise that there is a degree of uncertainty about the outcome of some events and other events are certain or impossible | Place events in order of likelihood and use appropriate words to identify the chance<br>Understand and use the idea of 'evens' and say whether events are more or less likely than this<br>Distinguish between 'fair' and 'unfair' |